marie claire

crisp

Published by Murdoch Books Pty Limited.

Murdoch Books Australia
Pier 8/9, 23 Hickson Rd
Millers Point NSW 2000
Phone: +61 (0)2 8220 2000
Fax: +61 (0)2 8220 2558

Murdoch Books UK Limited
Erico House, 6th Floor North
93–99 Upper Richmond Road
Putney, London SW15 2TG
Phone: +44 (0)20 8785 5995
Fax: +44 (0)20 8785 5985

Author and Stylist: Michele Cranston
Photographer: Petrina Tinslay
Design manager: Vivien Valk
Concept and design: Lauren Camilleri
Editor: Gordana Trifunovic
Food preparation: Ross Dobson and Jo Glynn
Production: Adele Troeger

Chief executive: Juliet Rogers
Publisher: Kay Scarlett

National Library of Australia Cataloguing-in-Publication Data
Cranston, Michele. Marie Claire crisp. Includes index.
ISBN 1 74045 672 6.
1. Cookery. I. Title. II. Title: Marie Claire (North Sydney, N.S.W.).   641.5

Printed by 1010 Printing International Ltd. Printed in China. First printed 2005.

Important: Those who might be at risk from the effects of salmonella poisoning (the elderly,
pregnant women, young children and those suffering from immune deficiency diseases) should
consult their doctor with any concerns about eating raw eggs.
Conversion guide: You may find cooking times vary depending on the oven you are using. For
fan-forced ovens, as a general rule, set the oven temperature to 20°C (35°F) lower than indicated
in the recipe. We have used 20 ml (4 teaspoon) tablespoon measures. If you are using a
15 ml (3 teaspoon) tablespoon, for most recipes the difference will not be noticeable. However, for
recipes using baking powder, gelatine, bicarbonate of soda (baking soda) or small amounts of flour
and cornflour, add an extra teaspoon for each tablespoon specified.

marie claire

crisp

michele cranston
photography by petrina tinslay

MURDOCH BOOKS

contents

Welcome to *marie claire crisp*, a selection of our favourite recipes that are crisp and cool, fresh and summery, with handfuls of herbs and leafy greens. A thick and hearty book with lots of yummy ideas which we hope will inspire you, with everything from leafy salads of crunch and colour to wintery vegetables tossed in seasoned oil, warming soups and syrupy baked apples.

I've had a lot of fun revisiting old favourites and I hope that you have as much fun cooking and eating from our selection.

michele cranston

ingredient note

lettuce

For me, salads are all about flavour and crunch. I can think of nothing better than sitting down to a bowl of some of my favourite ingredients tossed together with a lush array of leaves and the smooth bite of a good dressing. Nowadays with the supermarket aisles brimming with healthy bundles of leafy greens there really is no excuse not to enjoy such simple delights.

To enjoy these delicate leaves at their best there are a few simple rules to follow. Always buy lettuce that is in top condition. Avoid lettuce with spotted or mushy leaves and herbs that have begun to wilt. If possible rinse the greens in cold water when you get home. Drain well and place them into plastic crisper boxes or plastic bags in the refrigerator. Pre-picked leaves like rocket, English spinach, mizuna or mixed salad selections should be bought as close as possible to the day of use. Toss with a few select flavours like eggs, cheese, tinned tuna, olives, seasonal vegetables, cooked beans and lentils, chargrilled eggplant, marinated artichokes, roast peppers, crisp apple or fine sliced pear. The list of ingredients and possibilities are endless so just sit back and enjoy a healthy bowlful.

ingredient note

cucumber

Crisp and green with a watery crunch, cucumbers are a bite of summer. Indeed, it's hard to imagine any summer salad without them. Think the simplest of salads featuring lettuce, tomatoes and cucumbers through to Asian salads with soft strips of cucumber balancing the bite of chilli. Cucumbers are always perfect for introducing a cooling balance to hot dishes or salads with a little heat, or for providing a touch of lightness in a rich dish. Cut into chunks or julienned, they can be tossed through salads or puréed into the perfect soup for a hot midsummer evening. If you want elegant ribbons then use a vegetable peeler to remove paper-thin strips. Toss with finely chopped herbs and use as a base to a spicy fish dish. Finely chop and toss with yoghurt and mint for a smooth accompaniment to curries, or mix with a blend of herbs and avocado or tomato as a light summer salsa. There really are so many ways that they can be used to bring a lightness to summer recipes. If you wish to give the cucumbers a bit of body then remove the liquid content by cutting them to the required size, placing into a colander and sprinkling with salt. Allow the cucumber to sit for an hour then squeeze out the excess liquid. Fold through a little crème fraîche and serve with smoked fish.

herbs

Herbs bring with them a whole world of flavours. Sage, rosemary and oregano need to be used with a light touch. Tarragon, with its soft aniseed flavour, is wonderful scattered over a green salad or used to flavour sauces and dressings. Dill is marvelous with fish and potatoes, while chives can be sprinkled over anything that's leafy, eggy or fishy. Some herbs bring a lightness and freshness to certain recipes and these I tend to use by the handful. Lush and leafy parsley is welcome in almost any salad or richly flavoured meal. It's not too strong to overpower other flavours but still has enough freshness to lift the spirits of just about anything. Rocket has become a salad standard and can usually be bought as bunches of large leaves or as loose small leaves. Some varieties are particularly peppery and so should be mixed with other leaves or with strong flavours that will balance its bite. While coriander, with its particular flavour, is ideally suited to the vibrant ingredients found in Asian or Middle Eastern cuisines.

Whether cooked or scattered, enjoy herbs for the smile that they'll bring to your mouth.

green apples

Crunchy and green, juicy and sweet with just enough sour, green apples may make a delicious mouthful but they also make a fantastic base for many a classic dish. While apples are wonderful freshly sliced into a summery salad they really come into their own when cooked. It's no wonder that apple pie and Mom has become such a cliché since any dessert involving baked apples is instantly nostalgic and comforting. I have fond childhood memories of steamy bowls of stewed apples served with custard along with the distinct memories of fighting with my siblings for the curly green tails of skin that were peeled from the apples. Those slivers of green were a crunchy foretaste of good things to come.

Apples can be sliced over the top of a cake batter and sprinkled with cinnamon sugar, or baked with other fruits into a wintery crumble. They can be lightly stewed with a little orange juice and butter, or baked into a fluffy explosion of syrupy juices. Finely sliced, they can be fanned over puff pastry for a delicately perfect taste of apple, or richly caramelized to form the base of the justly famous Tarte Tatin. Add some dollops of cream, vanilla ice cream, caramel ice cream or home-made custard and who could stop at just one helping?

green papaya salad rice paper rolls fried green olives seared tuna with lime leaf and peanuts thai fish cakes salmon and chive fritters smoked trout and pickled cucumber on oatcakes pickled swordfish zucchini and marjoram frittatas lemon curry scallops cheese and olive sandwiches caper and polenta muffins with smoked salmon crab cocktail in a leaf salad of avocado and preserved lemon scallop and

01 starters and sides

coriander wontons crab with lemon, parsley and chilli lime and coconut pancakes with chicken and mint sage and polenta madeleines scallops with ginger and lemon grass caesar salad buttered roast asparagus cucumber tea-sandwiches oysters with lime green

steamed mussels with thai salsa

serves 4

2 kg (4 lb 8 oz) mussels in the shell
500 ml (17 fl oz/2 cups) white wine
2 tablespoons shaved palm sugar
   (jaggery)
1 tablespoon fish sauce
2 tablespoons lime juice
1 red chilli, seeded and thinly sliced
2 Lebanese (short) cucumbers,
   finely diced
1 tablespoon finely diced red
   capsicum (pepper)
15 mint leaves, thinly sliced
lime wedges, to serve

Clean the mussels in a sink filled with cold water, removing the beards and any barnacles from the shell. Discard any mussels that remain closed and don't open when you tap them. Put in a large lidded pot and pour over the wine. Cover with a tight-fitting lid and cook over high heat, shaking the pan occasionally. Check after 4 minutes, removing any mussels that have opened. If any stay closed, return them to the heat for a minute, then discard any that still haven't opened. Allow the mussels to cool.

Put the palm sugar, fish sauce and lime juice in a bowl and stir until the sugar has dissolved, then add the chilli, cucumber, capsicum and mint. Mix together. Break the top shells off the mussels so that the meat is left sitting on a half-shell. Arrange the mussels on a serving platter with lime wedges and spoon a little salsa into each one.

thai-style papaya salad

makes 20

1 small green papaya (approximately 250 g/9 oz)
1 red chilli, seeded and finely chopped
3 tablespoons lime juice
2 tablespoons fish sauce
3 tablespoons shaved palm sugar (jaggery)
2 garlic cloves, crushed
2 tablespoons dried Asian fried onions
4 large handfuls mint, roughly chopped
20 butter lettuce leaves, washed and drained

Coarsely grate the green papaya and set aside.

Make a sauce by combining the chilli, lime juice, fish sauce, palm sugar and garlic in a small bowl. Stir to dissolve the palm sugar.

Just prior to serving, combine the grated green papaya, fried onions, mint leaves and the dressing.

Place a tablespoon of the mixture in each of the lettuce leaves and serve.

rice paper rolls

1 handful coriander (cilantro) leaves
90 g (3¹/₄ oz/1 cup) freshly grated
    green papaya
45 g (1¹/₂ oz/¹/₂ cup) bean sprouts,
    roughly chopped
6 mint leaves, finely chopped
2 tablespoons finely diced red
    capsicum (pepper)
12 rice paper sheets
lime wedges, to serve

dipping sauce
1¹/₂ tablespoons sugar
3 tablespoons lime juice
1¹/₂ tablespoons fish sauce
¹/₂ garlic clove, finely chopped
1 small red chilli, seeded and
    finely chopped

To make the dipping sauce, combine the sugar, lime juice, fish sauce, garlic and chilli in a small bowl. Stir until the sugar has dissolved. Set aside.

Put the coriander leaves, green papaya, bean sprouts, mint leaves and capsicum in a bowl and stir to combine.

Fill a large bowl with warm water and soak one of the rice paper sheets until it is just soft. Remove to a clean work surface and place a spoonful of mixture into the lower section of the sheet. Fold the two sides over so that they slightly overlap, then roll the sheet up. You should have a neat parcel. Set aside and repeat with the remaining rice sheets. Serve the rolls with the dipping sauce.

fried green olives

2 tablespoons finely chopped flat-leaf (Italian) parsley

50 g (1³/4 oz/¹/3 cup) crumbled feta cheese

20 large green olives, pitted

30 g (1 oz/¹/4 cup) plain (all-purpose) flour

1 egg, beaten

50 g (1³/4 oz/¹/2 cup) fine breadcrumbs

100 ml (3¹/2 fl oz) vegetable oil

Place the parsley and feta in a bowl and stir well, then stuff a little of the mixture into the centre of each of the olives.

Place the flour in a shallow bowl, the egg in a small bowl and the breadcrumbs in another bowl. Heat the oil in a deep frying pan over medium heat. Toss the olives, a few at a time, in the flour, then dip into the beaten egg and finally roll in the breadcrumbs. Fry in the oil for 1 minute, or until golden brown. Remove from the pan and drain on paper towels. Repeat with the remaining olives.

seared tuna with lime leaf and peanuts
makes 30

50 ml (1³/₄ fl oz) tamarind water (basics)
1 tablespoon roughly chopped palm sugar (jaggery)
4 tablespoons lime juice
1 tablespoon grated fresh ginger
1 tablespoon fish sauce
2 teaspoons sesame oil
1 red chilli, seeded and finely chopped
1 tablespoon finely chopped makrut (kaffir lime) leaves
1 tablespoon finely chopped lemon grass, white part only
vegetable oil, for cooking
300 g (10¹/₂ oz) tuna fillet, cut into small pieces
3 thin Lebanese (short) cucumbers
1 large handful coriander (cilantro) leaves
80 g (2³/₄ oz/¹/₂ cup) peanuts, toasted and finely chopped

Place the tamarind water, palm sugar, lime juice, ginger, fish sauce, sesame oil, chilli, makrut leaves and lemon grass in a small bowl and stir well to dissolve the palm sugar.

Lightly oil a frying pan, place over high heat and sear the tuna fillets for 1 minute on each side. Remove from the heat and season with a little sea salt. Slice the cucumbers into 5 mm– 1 cm (¹/₄–¹/₂ in) rounds and top with a slice of tuna. Toss the coriander leaves and peanuts through the dressing and place a teaspoon of dressing onto each of the tuna slices. Serve immediately.

thai fish cakes

makes 20

450 g (1 lb) red snapper fillets
2 tablespoons fish sauce
1 tablespoon red curry paste
1 egg
1 teaspoon shaved palm sugar
   (jaggery)
3 thinly sliced makrut (kaffir lime)
   leaves
70 g (2¹/2 oz) green beans
1 large red chilli
sunflower oil, for cooking
sweet chilli sauce, to serve

Put the red snapper fillets into a food processor with the fish sauce, curry paste, egg, palm sugar and makrut leaves and process until smooth. Thinly slice the beans into rounds. Remove the seeds from the chilli and finely chop the chilli. Stir the beans and chilli into the puréed fish.

Roll 1 heaped tablespoon of mixture into a ball and then flatten it a little. Set aside and repeat with the remaining mixture. Heat the oil in a large frying pan over medium to high heat and fry the fish cakes, a few at a time, until golden brown on both sides. Drain on paper towels. Serve with sweet chilli sauce.

pickled swordfish

50 ml (1³/4 fl oz) olive oil

2 red onions, thinly sliced

1–2 small red chillies, seeded
and finely chopped

2 garlic cloves, crushed

300 g (10¹/2 oz) ripe tomatoes,
finely diced

1 teaspoon sea salt

400 g (14 oz) swordfish fillets, boned,
skin removed, and finely diced

3 handfuls mint

4 lemons, juiced

20 baby mignonette or cos (romaine)
lettuce leaves, washed and drained

Heat the olive oil in a frying pan over medium heat, add the onions and gently cook for 5–7 minutes, stirring, until soft and transparent. Stir through the chillies, garlic, tomatoes and sea salt. Remove from the heat and set aside to cool.

Place the raw fish pieces in a single layer in a wide ceramic or glass dish. Cover with the onion mixture and fresh mint and pour over enough lemon juice to cover all the ingredients. Cover and leave to marinate in the refrigerator for 24 hours. To serve, place a small amount of pickled fish in the centre of each lettuce leaf and season with a sprinkle of sea salt and some freshly ground black pepper.

smoked trout and pickled cucumber on oatcakes makes 24

2 Lebanese (short) cucumbers, sliced
  in half lengthways
2 tablespoons lemon juice
200 g (7 oz) smoked trout, flaked
90 g (3¹/₄ oz/¹/₃ cup) sour cream
1 tablespoon finely chopped lemon
  zest
3 teaspoons dill
24 oatcakes (basics)

Use a teaspoon to scoop out the seeds from the cucumbers. Thinly slice, then sprinkle the flesh with 1 teaspoon of salt. Place in a sieve over a bowl and leave for 1 hour. Squeeze the cucumber of all liquid, then pat dry with paper towels. Place in a bowl, add 2 teaspoons of the lemon juice and mix.

In another bowl, combine the trout, sour cream and lemon zest. Season with salt and freshly ground black pepper and add the remaining lemon juice, tasting as you go. Place a teaspoon of the trout mixture onto each of the oatcakes and top with a little of the cucumber. Sprinkle with dill.

salmon and chive fritters

makes 36

250 g (9 oz) salmon fillet, boned and
    skin removed
3 teaspoons finely chopped lemon zest
2 eggs, lightly beaten
125 g (4¹/₂ oz/1 cup) plain (all-purpose)
    flour
1 teaspoon baking powder
2 tablespoons plain yoghurt
60 g (2¹/₄ oz/¹/₂ cup) thinly sliced
    garlic chives
65 g (2¹/₄ oz/1 cup) thinly sliced spring
    onions (scallions)
vegetable oil, for cooking
lemon wedges, to serve

Slice the salmon to form 1 cm (¹/₂ in) dice. Place in a small bowl, cover and refrigerate until ready to use.

Place the zest, eggs, flour, baking powder and yoghurt in a bowl and whisk until smooth. Just prior to cooking, fold the salmon, garlic chives and spring onions through the batter until evenly mixed. Season well with salt and freshly ground black pepper.

Heat a large frying pan over medium heat and add a tablespoon of oil. Place heaped teaspoons of the mixture into the pan and press down to form flat fritters. As each fritter becomes golden on the bottom, turn and cook until golden on both sides. Remove and drain on paper towels. Repeat this process, adding a little more oil to the frying pan as necessary. Serve warm accompanied by lemon wedges.

zucchini and marjoram frittatas

makes 24

20 g (3/4 oz) butter
1 red onion, thinly sliced
1 teaspoon finely chopped marjoram
205 g (71/4 oz/11/2 cups) grated
   zucchini (courgette)
6 eggs
50 g (13/4 oz/1/2 cup) grated fresh
   parmesan cheese

Preheat the oven to 180°C (350°F/ Gas 4). Heat the butter in a frying pan and sauté the onion and marjoram over medium heat for 7–10 minutes, or until the onion is soft and caramelized. Spoon the mixture into two lightly greased, shallow, 12-holed patty cake tins. Top with the grated zucchini. Whisk the eggs with a tablespoon of water and season with salt and ground white pepper. Fill each of the patty tins with the egg mixture and sprinkle with the parmesan. Bake for 10 minutes, or until set.

lemon curry scallops

serves 4

5 g (1/8 oz) butter
2 French shallots, finely diced
1 teaspoon green curry paste
1 tablespoon finely chopped lemon
   grass, white part only
150 ml (5 fl oz) coconut cream
1 lemon, juiced
16 scallops on the shell, cleaned
1 handful coriander (cilantro) leaves,
   to serve
lime wedges, to serve

Put the butter, shallots, curry paste and lemon grass into a small saucepan over low to medium heat. Cook for 3 minutes. Add the coconut cream and simmer for 2 minutes before stirring in the lemon juice.

Place the scallops, still in their shells, under a grill (broiler) for 2–3 minutes. Spoon a little of the creamy sauce over each scallop. Serve with a scattering of coriander leaves and lime wedges.

cheese and olive sandwiches

makes 12 small slices

40 g (1¹/2 oz/¹/3 cup) pitted and thinly
sliced green olives
100 g (3¹/2 oz/²/3 cup) grated
mozzarella cheese
30 g (1 oz/heaped ¹/4 cup) grated fresh
parmesan cheese
2 tablespoons roughly chopped
flat-leaf (Italian) parsley
8 slices white bread, crusts removed
2 tablespoons olive oil

Preheat the oven to 180°C (350°F/
Gas 4). Place the olives, mozzarella,
parmesan and parsley in a bowl and
mix well to combine. Brush four slices
of bread with half the olive oil and
place them, oiled side down, on a
greased baking tray. Divide the cheese
mixture evenly among the four slices
of bread and top with the remaining
four slices. Brush the tops of the
sandwiches with the remaining oil and
place in the oven for 10 minutes,
turning if necessary. Remove and slice
each piece into three fingers.

caper and polenta muffins
with smoked salmon   makes 18

185 g (6 1/2 oz/1 1/2 cups) plain
   (all-purpose) flour
100 g (3 1/2 oz/2/3 cup) polenta
2 teaspoons baking powder
2 tablespoons salted capers, rinsed
   and drained
1 large handful roughly chopped
   flat-leaf (Italian) parsley
1/2 teaspoon finely chopped tarragon
250 ml (9 fl oz/1 cup) milk
2 tablespoons olive oil
1 egg
90 g (3 1/4 oz/1/3 cup) sour cream
180 g (6 oz) smoked salmon
wasabi roe or fresh dill, to garnish

Preheat the oven to 180°C (350°F/
Gas 4). Place the flour, polenta, baking
powder, capers, parsley and tarragon
in a bowl and mix well. Season with
some freshly ground black pepper. In a
jug, whisk together the milk, oil and
egg. Pour into the bowl of dry
ingredients and fold through until
just combined. Spoon the mixture into
a greased patty tin and bake for
20 minutes. When completely cool, cut
off the tops of the muffins. Top the
muffins with sour cream and about
10 g (1/4 oz) of smoked salmon per
muffin. Garnish with wasabi roe or
fresh dill.

crab cocktail in a leaf

makes 16-20

2 egg yolks
1 lemon, zested and juiced
250 ml (9 fl oz/1 cup) light olive oil
1 teaspoon Dijon mustard
2 teaspoons finely chopped tarragon
1 tablespoon tomato paste
   (concentrated purée)
250 g (9 oz) fresh cooked crab meat
16–20 baby gem lettuce leaves
Tabasco sauce, to serve

Whisk the egg yolks, lemon zest and juice together. Slowly drizzle in the oil, whisking the mixture until it becomes thick and creamy. Fold in the mustard, tarragon and tomato paste. Set aside. Break up the crab meat with a fork, leaving it in fairly large pieces, then fold it into the dressing and season well. Spoon the crab into the baby gem leaves and top each with a dash of Tabasco.

salad of avocado and preserved lemon

serves 6

2 avocados
3 Lebanese (short) cucumbers
2 tablespoons finely chopped
  preserved lemon
4 tablespoons coriander (cilantro),
  roughly chopped
2 tablespoons virgin olive oil
1 tablespoon lemon juice

Remove the skin and stone from the avocados. Cut into bite-sized chunks. Halve the cucumbers lengthways and slice them into thick pieces on the diagonal.

Put the avocados, cucumber, preserved lemon, coriander, olive oil and lemon juice in a bowl and lightly toss together without breaking up the avocado. Serve with fish or as a side salad.

scallop and coriander wontons

makes 30

400 g (14 oz) white scallop meat, finely diced
1/2 teaspoon grated orange zest
15 g (1/2 oz/1/4 cup) thinly sliced spring onions (scallions)
3 tablespoons finely chopped coriander (cilantro) leaves
1/4 teaspoon sesame oil
2 teaspoons finely chopped red chillies
1 teaspoon fish sauce
1 makrut (kaffir lime) leaf, shredded
1/4 teaspoon grated fresh ginger
2 tablespoons plain (all-purpose) flour
1 egg
30 square wonton wrappers
peanut oil, for deep-frying
lime wedges, to serve

Combine the scallop meat, zest, spring onions, coriander, sesame oil, chilli, fish sauce, makrut leaf and ginger in a bowl. Sprinkle the flour over the top, season and stir well. Lightly beat the egg with 60 ml (2 fl oz/1/4 cup) of water. Place a wonton wrapper on a clean surface and place 1 heaped teaspoon of the scallop mixture into the centre. Brush the egg wash along the edges. Bring the corners together, sealing the sides, then twist the top firmly. Repeat with the remaining mixture. Heat the oil in a wok and cook the wontons, in batches, until golden brown. Remove and serve with lime wedges.

crab with lemon, parsley and chilli on toasts makes 40

10 slices white bread, crusts removed
50 ml (1³/₄ fl oz) olive oil
250 g (9 oz) fresh cooked crab meat, shredded
2 tablespoons grated lemon zest
1 tablespoon virgin olive oil
1 small red chilli, seeded and finely chopped
2 tablespoons finely chopped flat-leaf (Italian) parsley
2 teaspoons lemon juice
40 basil leaves

Preheat the oven to 160°C (315°F/ Gas 2–3). Cut each slice of bread into four circles using a cookie cutter. Place on a baking tray, lightly brush with olive oil and bake until golden brown. Allow to cool. Place the crab meat in a bowl, add the remaining ingredients and stir well to combine. Place a basil leaf onto each of the little toasts and top with a heaped teaspoon of the crab mix. Serve immediately.

Note – This mix will keep well for several hours, so it is an easy one to prepare in advance.

lime and coconut pancakes with chicken and mint makes 20

170 ml (5¹/2 fl oz/²/3 cup) lime juice

2 teaspoons sesame oil

2 tablespoons shaved palm sugar (jaggery)

2 teaspoons fish sauce

1 teaspoon seeded and finely chopped red chilli

400 g (14 oz) chicken, poached and shredded

125 g (4¹/2 oz/1 cup) plain (all-purpose) flour

1 egg, lightly beaten

1 lime, zested and juiced

250 ml (9 fl oz/1 cup) coconut milk

1 large handful mint

3 handfuls coriander (cilantro) leaves

Combine the lime juice, sesame oil, sugar, fish sauce and chilli in a bowl and stir to dissolve the sugar. Add the chicken.

Make the pancakes by sifting the flour and 1/4 teaspoon of salt into a bowl. Make a well in the centre and stir in the egg, zest, juice and coconut milk. Whisk to form a smooth batter. Grease a large non-stick frying pan and heat over low heat. Drizzle in the batter in a cobweb of lines, making a circle 10 cm (4 in) in diameter. Leave to cook for 2 minutes, then flip and cook for a further 1–2 minutes, or until golden. Transfer to a plate and repeat with the remaining pancake mixture. Prior to serving, toss the mint and coriander leaves through the chicken. Fill each of the pancakes with some of the chicken salad. Roll up and serve immediately.

walnut crisps with creamed goat's cheese and pear makes 50

150 g (5¹/₂ oz) fresh goat's cheese
125 ml (4 fl oz/¹/₂ cup) cream
  (whipping)
50 pieces walnut bread (basics)
2 ripe pears

Mix the goat's cheese and cream together, and season with salt and freshly ground black pepper. To assemble, spread a small amount of the goat's cheese mixture on top of each slice of walnut bread. Cut the pears into thin wedges and place on top of the goat's cheese.

sage and polenta madeleines

makes 24

150 g (5¹/2 oz) unsalted butter, softened
2 teaspoons sugar
2 egg yolks
2 eggs
40 g (1¹/2 oz/¹/3 cup) plain (all-purpose) flour
50 g (1³/4 oz/¹/3 cup) fine polenta
1¹/4 teaspoons baking powder
1¹/4 teaspoons salt
1¹/4 teaspoons coarsely ground black pepper
24 small sage leaves

Preheat the oven to 180°C (350°F/ Gas 4). Place 30 g (1 oz) of the butter in a small saucepan and cook over high heat until it begins to brown. Remove from the heat and set aside. Cream the remaining butter and the sugar in a mixing bowl until pale and fluffy. Gradually add the yolks and whole eggs, beating well after each addition. Slowly fold in the dry ingredients, plus the salt and coarsely ground black pepper.

Grease a madeleine tin with the browned butter, place a sage leaf in the base of each mould and top with a teaspoon of batter. If you don't have a madeleine tin, use shallow muffin or patty cake tins. Bake for 7–10 minutes, or until the cakes are golden and springy to the touch. Remove from the tray and cool on a wire rack.

scallops with ginger and lemon grass

serves 4

2 tablespoons finely chopped lemon
   grass, white part only
2 teaspoons grated fresh ginger
1/2 red chilli, seeded and finely
   chopped
1 tablespoon sesame oil
2 tablespoons mirin
1 tablespoon fish sauce
1 lime, juiced
12 scallops on the shell, cleaned
coriander (cilantro) leaves, to serve
lime wedges, to serve

Mix together the lemon grass, ginger, chilli, sesame oil, mirin, fish sauce and lime juice and leave to infuse for a few minutes.

Spoon a little of the marinade over each of the scallops and arrange them, still in their shells, in one or two steamer baskets. Put the steamer baskets over a saucepan of simmering water. Cover and steam for 4 minutes, swapping the baskets after 2 minutes. Remove the scallops from the baskets without letting any of the juices escape from the shells and serve them with a sprinkle of coriander and lime wedges.

caesar salad cups

makes approximately 24

10 slices white bread, crusts removed
1 garlic clove, crushed
15 g (1/2 oz) anchovies, shredded
1 egg yolk
1/2 teaspoon Worcestershire sauce
2 tablespoons lemon juice
185 ml (6 fl oz/3/4 cup) vegetable or
    light olive oil
50 g (13/4 oz/1/2 cup) grated fresh
    parmesan cheese
3 mignonette lettuces, leaves washed
    and drained

Preheat the oven to 150°C (300°F/ Gas 2). Slice the bread into 5 mm (1/4 in) cubes. Place on a baking tray and toast in the oven until golden. Allow the croutons to cool.

Place the garlic, anchovies, egg yolk, Worcestershire sauce, lemon juice and some freshly ground black pepper in a bowl and blend together. Whisk the mixture continuously while slowly pouring in the oil to form a thick mayonnaise. Fold the parmesan and croutons through the mayonnaise.

Thinly slice any large lettuce leaves and add them to the mayonnaise. Spoon the mixture into the small lettuce leaves and serve immediately.

spinach, black bean and orange wontons

makes 24

1 kg (2 lb 4 oz) English spinach
grated zest of 1 orange
3 tablespoons Chinese salted
  black beans
1 tablespoon shaved palm sugar
  (jaggery)
1 tablespoon Chinese rice wine
1/2 teaspoon sesame oil
24 square wonton wrappers
sweet chilli sauce, to serve

Blanch the spinach until emerald green. Drain and set aside to cool. Finely chop the spinach leaves and put them in a bowl with the zest and black beans. Put the palm sugar, Chinese rice wine and sesame oil into a small bowl. Stir until the sugar has dissolved and then pour the sauce over the spinach. Stir to combine the filling ingredients.

Put 1 wonton wrapper on a clean surface and moisten the edge with a little water. Put 1 heaped teaspoon of the filling mixture in the centre, bring the four corners together and pinch to seal the edges. Put onto a tray lined with baking paper. Repeat with the remaining mixture. Steam for 10–12 minutes and serve with sweet chilli sauce.

buttered roast asparagus

serves 4

60 g (2¹/₄ oz) butter
350 g (12 oz) thin asparagus spears,
    trimmed
4 slices wholemeal (whole-wheat) toast
1 lemon
30 g (1 oz/¹/₃ cup) shaved fresh
    parmesan cheese

Preheat the oven to 180°C (350°F/ Gas 4). Put a roasting tin over low heat and add the butter. When the butter has melted, add the asparagus. Season with a little salt and pepper. Roll the asparagus around so that it is well coated in the butter and then put the asparagus in the oven to roast for 10 minutes.

Arrange the toast on four plates and top each with some asparagus. Squeeze a little lemon juice into the roasting tin, swirl it around and then drizzle the pan juices over the asparagus. Top with the parmesan.

fennel and grapefruit salad with rich apple dressing

serves 4

500 ml (17 fl oz/2 cups) apple juice
3 black peppercorns
2 sprigs thyme
1 tablespoon balsamic vinegar
1 teaspoon celery salt
2 fennel bulbs, trimmed, very
thinly sliced
2 pink grapefruits, peeled and
segments removed
2 celery stalks, thinly sliced

To make the rich apple dressing, put the apple juice, peppercorns and thyme into a small saucepan and place over medium heat. Bring to the boil and reduce until the liquid is syrupy and there is approximately 60 ml (2 fl oz/1/4 cup). Set aside and allow to cool. Add the balsamic vinegar and celery salt to the syrup. Stir to combine. Pile the fennel, grapefruit and celery on a serving platter and drizzle with the dressing. Season with salt and freshly ground black pepper. Serve with cold roast pork or chicken.

cucumber tea-sandwiches

makes 18 small slices

2 tablespoons finely chopped dill
50 g (1³/4 oz) butter, softened, or
 60 g (2¹/4 oz/¹/4 cup) mayonnaise
12 thin slices bread, crusts removed
2 Lebanese (short) cucumbers,
 thinly sliced

Fold the dill through the softened butter or mayonnaise and spread lightly onto the slices of bread. Place the thinly sliced cucumber on six of the bread slices. Season with freshly ground black pepper and top with the remaining bread. Cut each sandwich into three fingers. Serve immediately.

oysters with lime

1 tablespoon lime juice
1 teaspoon black sesame seeds
1/4 teaspoon sesame oil
1 tablespoon finely diced Lebanese
   (short) cucumber
2 dozen freshly shucked oysters

Combine the lime juice, sesame seeds, oil and cucumber in a small bowl. Serve the oysters accompanied by the dressing.

whitebait fritters

125 g (4¹/₂ oz/1 cup) plain (all-purpose)
  flour
¹/₂ teaspoon cayenne pepper
1 teaspoon grated lemon zest
1 egg
20 g (³/₄ oz) butter, melted
3 tablespoons milk
250 g (9 oz) small whitebait
3 tablespoons finely chopped flat-leaf
  (Italian) parsley
vegetable oil, for frying
lime wedges, to serve

Put the flour into a food processor. Add the cayenne pepper, lemon zest, egg, butter, 1 teaspoon of salt and milk. Process to form a thick batter. Spoon into a bowl and stir in the whitebait and parsley. Heat some vegetable oil in a deep heavy-based frying pan over medium heat. To test if the oil is sizzling hot, drop in a little batter, then drop small spoonfuls of the batter into the oil and fry on each side until golden brown. Remove and drain on paper towels. Serve while warm, with lime wedges.

fennel remoulade

serves 4

2 egg yolks
1 lemon, juiced
250 ml (9 fl oz/1 cup) oil
1 tablespoon Dijon mustard
3 large fennel bulbs, trimmed
1 handful flat-leaf (Italian) parsley
4 slices heavy rye bread, toasted

Whisk the egg yolks and lemon juice together in a bowl. Slowly drizzle in the oil, whisking, until the mixture becomes thick and creamy. Stir in the mustard and season to taste with sea salt. Set the mayonnaise aside.

Slice the fennel into paper-thin slices, then chop. Add to the mayonnaise and stir until the fennel is well coated, then add the parsley. Serve with rye toast.

mozzarella cheese, artichoke and parsley crostini   makes 12

175 g (6 oz) jar marinated artichoke
  hearts
1 tablespoon roughly chopped flat-leaf
  (Italian) parsley, plus extra to serve
1 baguette
olive oil, for brushing
100 g (3 1/2 oz) fresh mozzarella
  cheese, thinly sliced
extra virgin olive oil, for drizzlng

Preheat the oven to 150°C (300°F/ Gas 2). Drain the artichoke hearts and put them into a food processor with the flat-leaf parsley. Season with a little ground white pepper and process to a smooth paste. Cut the baguette into 12 thin slices and brush one side of each slice with olive oil. Put the slices on a baking tray and bake until golden brown, turning them once. Remove from the oven and spread the artichoke paste on top of the crostini slices. Top with the mozzarella cheese and garnish with a parsley leaf and a light drizzle of extra virgin olive oil.

steamed salmon with fennel and mint

makes 20

2 teaspoons mustard seeds
1/2 teaspoon fennel seeds
2 teaspoons sugar
2 tablespoons olive oil
1/2 teaspoon white vinegar
140 g (5 oz/1 cup) coarsely grated fennel
175 g (6 oz) Lebanese (short) cucumber, thinly sliced
20 g (3/4 oz) thinly sliced mint
4 tablespoons lemon juice
200 g (7 oz) salmon fillet, boned and skin removed
20 scallop shells or Chinese spoons, for serving

Place the mustard and fennel seeds, the sugar and 1/4 teaspoon of salt in a mortar and pestle and grind until the fennel seeds have been crushed. Add the oil and vinegar and stir to form a thick dressing. Combine the fennel, cucumber, mint and lemon juice in a bowl. Pour the dressing over the salad and mix well.

Slice the salmon into ten thin strips and then slice each in half again, giving you twenty 8 cm x 4 cm x 5 mm (31/4 x 11/2 x 1/4 in) pieces. Place a piece of salmon on each of the shells or spoons. Place in a bamboo steamer over a saucepan of boiling water. Cover and steam for 2 minutes. Remove from the basket and top with the fennel salad. Serve immediately.

avocado on sourdough serves 4

8 slices thickly cut sourdough
1 garlic clove, lightly crushed
4 vine-ripened tomatoes, sliced
2 avocados, cut into wedges
2 tablespoons extra virgin olive oil

Lightly toast the sourdough bread on one side, then rub the garlic clove over the toasted surface. Arrange the tomato slices over the bread and top with some thick wedges of avocado. Season liberally with sea salt and freshly ground black pepper. Drizzle with the olive oil and serve.

orange and watercress salad

3 leeks, trimmed
2 tablespoons olive oil
3 teaspoons soy sauce
3 oranges, peeled and thinly sliced
    into rings
400 g (14 oz) watercress, picked over
2 tablespoons extra virgin olive oil

Slice the leeks in half lengthways, then rinse well in a large bowl of cold water. Cut the leeks into 3 cm (1 1/4 in) lengths and thinly slice. Put into a large saucepan with the olive oil over medium heat. Cover and simmer for 10 minutes, or until the leeks are soft. Drizzle with the soy sauce, remove and allow to cool. Layer the orange slices with the watercress and leeks. Drizzle with a little olive oil and season with freshly ground black pepper.

chicken and herb tea-sandwiches

makes 24 triangles

300 g (10½ oz) boneless, skinless
  chicken thigh
1 handful flat-leaf (Italian) parsley,
  roughly chopped
2 teaspoons olive oil
1 teaspoon thyme
2 teaspoons finely chopped chives
2 teaspoons finely chopped mint
50 g (1¾ oz) butter, softened
12 thin slices white bread, crusts
  removed

Preheat the oven to 180°C (350°F/ Gas 4). Place the chicken and parsley on a small baking tray, pour over the oil and sprinkle with thyme and 1 teaspoon of salt. Cover with foil and bake for 30 minutes. Allow the chicken to cool, then finely chop or shred the flesh. Fold the chives and mint through the softened butter and spread lightly onto the slices of bread. Divide the chicken equally between six slices of bread, season with salt and freshly ground black pepper and top with the remaining bread slices. Cut the sandwiches into four triangles. Serve immediately.

sashimi tuna with spinach and sesame

makes 30

200 g (7 oz) sashimi tuna
250 g (9 oz) English spinach, rinsed and stalks removed
1 teaspoon caster (superfine) sugar
2 tablespoons soy sauce
50 g (1 3/4 oz/1/3 cup) sesame seeds
2 teaspoons mirin

Place the tuna in the freezer for 30–35 minutes. (This firms the tuna flesh, making it easier to slice thinly.) Plunge the spinach leaves into salted boiling water for 20 seconds, then remove and place in a bowl of iced water. Drain and squeeze out any excess water before shredding finely.

In a small bowl, dissolve the sugar in the soy sauce. Toast the sesame seeds in a frying pan over medium heat, removing from the heat when they begin to pop. Roughly grind or chop the seeds. Place them in a small bowl along with the mirin, soy sauce and sugar mixture, and the spinach. With a sharp knife, slice the tuna very thinly to make approximately 30 slices. Place one of the slices onto a clean work surface. Take a teaspoon of the spinach, squeeze it of any liquid and place it at one end of the tuna. Roll up and place on a serving platter. Repeat with the remaining tuna and spinach. Serve immediately.

guacamole

serves 4-6

1 red chilli, seeded and finely chopped
2 limes, juiced
3 tablespoons olive oil
2 spring onions (scallions), thinly sliced
3 tablespoons finely chopped
  coriander (cilantro) leaves
1 Lebanese (short) cucumber, finely
  diced
1 ripe tomato
2 avocados

Put the chilli in a bowl. Add the lime juice, olive oil, spring onions, coriander leaves and cucumber. Cut the tomato in half, scoop out the seeds and finely dice the flesh. Add the tomato flesh to the bowl and stir the ingredients together. Cut the avocados in half and remove the stones. With a small sharp knife, cut the flesh into a fine dice with crisscrossing lines. Run a large spoon between the skin and the flesh and scoop out the diced avocado. Add to the bowl and lightly fold to combine. Serve with corn chips or toasted tortilla triangles.

bean salad

3 tablespoons extra virgin olive oil
1 tablespoon lemon juice
1 teaspoon walnut oil
1/2 teaspoon caster (superfine) sugar
1/2 teaspoon Dijon mustard
400 g (14 oz) green beans, trimmed
400 g (14 oz) tin butterbeans (lima beans), drained and rinsed
1 handful flat-leaf (Italian) parsley, chopped

Put the extra virgin olive oil, lemon juice, walnut oil, sugar and mustard in a large bowl and season liberally with freshly ground black pepper and sea salt. Whisk with a fork until combined. Blanch the green beans in boiling water until they begin to turn bright green, then quickly drain and add to the bowl. Toss the green beans until they are well coated in the dressing. Allow to cool, then add the butter beans and parsley and toss again. Serve with seared tuna or barbecued steaks.

asparagus with lemon crumbs

serves 4

2 slices wholemeal (whole-wheat)
  bread
1 garlic clove
1 teaspoon sea salt
1 teaspoon thyme
1/2 teaspoon roughly chopped
  rosemary
1 lemon, zested and juiced
1 tablespoon olive oil
465 g (1 lb) asparagus, trimmed
50 g (13/4 oz) unsalted butter, chilled
  and cut into cubes
40 g (11/2 oz/heaped 1/3 cup) finely
  grated fresh parmesan cheese

Preheat the oven to 200°C (400°F/ Gas 6). Remove the crusts and put the bread into a food processor with the garlic, sea salt, thyme, rosemary, lemon zest and olive oil. Process until breadcrumbs form. Scatter the crumbs on a shallow tray and bake in the oven until golden brown.

Blanch the asparagus until it is bright green, then drain and refresh in cold water. Put the lemon juice in a small saucepan over medium heat. Whisk in the cold butter. Remove from the heat when the butter is melted.

Divide the asparagus between four small plates and sprinkle with the breadcrumbs and parmesan cheese. Drizzle with the warm lemon sauce and serve immediately.

nori salsa

1 Lebanese (short) cucumber, finely
  julienned
1/2 daikon, julienned
1 tablespoon finely chopped pickled
  ginger
a few drops of sesame oil
1/2 teaspoon red chilli powder
1 tablespoon rice vinegar
2 teaspoons sesame seeds, toasted
1 nori sheet

Add the cucumber to a bowl with the daikon, ginger, sesame oil, chilli powder, rice wine vinegar and sesame seeds. Preheat the oven to 180°C (350°F/ Gas 4) oven. Take the nori sheet and lightly toast in the oven until crisp. Using a pair of kitchen scissors, cut the toasted nori sheet into thin julienne strips approximately 3 cm (1 1/4 in) long. Add the strips to the other ingredients. Gently toss to combine. Serve with rice or grilled (broiled) chicken or thinly sliced rare roasted beef.

soy beef fillet with pickled ginger

makes 15-20

300 g (10¹/2 oz) beef fillet, trimmed
3 tablespoons soy sauce
3 tablespoons mirin
1 tablespoon vegetable oil
90 g (3¹/4 oz/1 cup) shredded daikon
90 g (3¹/4 oz/¹/2 cup) shredded
   cucumber
1 teaspoon grated fresh ginger
1 teaspoon sesame oil
1 nori sheet
2 tablespoons pickled ginger

Cut the beef fillet in half lengthways. Place 2 tablespoons each of the soy sauce and mirin into a ceramic dish. Add the beef and cover and marinate in the fridge overnight, turning the beef occasionally.

Heat the oil in a frying pan over high heat. Sear the beef for several minutes on each side. Season with sea salt and freshly ground black pepper. Cover with foil and allow to cool.

Place the daikon, cucumber, fresh ginger, sesame oil and the remaining tablespoon each of soy sauce and mirin in a bowl and toss together. Slice the nori sheet into 2 cm (³/4 in) wide strips and then cut each strip in half.

Slice the beef very thinly. Place a little of the daikon salad and a small piece of pickled ginger onto one of the beef slices and roll it up. Place it onto a strip of nori and roll again. Place the parcel onto a plate with the loose end of the nori facing down. Repeat with the remaining ingredients. Serve at room temperature.

seared beef with rocket

makes 20

350 g (12 oz) beef fillet, trimmed
1 tablespoon olive oil
20 large rocket (arugula) leaves
100 g (3¹/2 oz/heaped ¹/3 cup) pesto
   (basics)

Rub 1 tablespoon of freshly ground black pepper into the surface of the beef fillet. Heat the oil in a frying pan over high heat and sear the fillet for 4 minutes on each side, or until nicely coloured. Remove, season with salt, cover with foil and, when cool, slice into 20 very thin slices.

Place the rocket leaves onto a clean surface. On top of each one place a thin slice of beef. Add a teaspoon of pesto and roll up. Serve immediately.

polenta and zucchini salad with blue cheese dressing

serves 4

75 g (2¹/2 oz/¹/2 cup) polenta
10 g (¹/4 oz) butter
6 zucchini (courgettes), sliced on the diagonal
3 tablespoons olive oil
2 tablespoons blue cheese, crumbled
4 tablespoons extra virgin olive oil
1 tablespoon red wine vinegar
150 g (5¹/2 oz) baby English spinach

Preheat the oven to 200°C (400°F/ Gas 6). Bring 350 ml (12 fl oz) of salted water to the boil in a large saucepan. Slowly pour in the polenta and stir until the polenta thickens and begins to draw away from the sides of the saucepan. Stir in the butter then remove from the heat. Pour the polenta onto a tray or flat plate until 1 cm (¹/2 in) thick. Allow to cool.

Put the zucchini on a baking tray and brush with a little of the olive oil. Bake until soft and cooked through. Slice the cooled polenta into rectangular chips and put on an oiled tray. Brush the polenta with a little oil and bake for 10 minutes.

To make the blue cheese dressing, combine the blue cheese, extra virgin olive oil and vinegar in a small bowl. Layer the zucchini, polenta and spinach onto four serving plates and drizzle with the dressing.

lemon grass prawns

20 small bamboo skewers
2 lemon grass stems, trimmed and
    roughly chopped
1 handful coriander (cilantro) leaves
4 tablespoons ground rice
1 tablespoon shaved palm sugar
    (jaggery)
2 tablespoons lime juice
20 raw king prawns (shrimp), peeled
    and deveined with tails intact
lime wedges, to serve

Put the bamboo skewers in a bowl of cold water to soak.

Put the lemon grass, coriander, ground rice, palm sugar and lime juice in a food processor. Process to form a thick paste. Set aside.

Open out the prawn along the incision along the back by lightly flattening it with the palm of your hand. Press 1 teaspoon of the lemon grass paste along this surface, then skewer the prawn around the paste so that the paste is held in place. When all the prawns are ready, lightly grill them on a barbecue or cook in a frying pan. Cook the prawns on each side for a few minutes or until they are orange and the flesh is opaque. Serve with lime wedges.

caramelized fennel
and apple

serves 4

20 g (³/₄ oz) butter
1 small fennel bulb, thinly sliced
20 sage leaves
2 green apples, cored and thinly sliced
3 tablespoons white wine
1 teaspoon sugar

Melt the butter in a large heavy-based pan over medium heat. Add the fennel. Sauté the fennel until it is golden and soft, then add the sage leaves and cook for a minute. Season with sea salt and white pepper before adding the apple, white wine and sugar.

Cover and cook for a few minutes until the apples are just beginning to soften and caramelize. Be careful not to let them get too dark. Serve with grilled pork chops or roast pork loin.

bean and pistachio salad

300 g (10¹/2 oz) green beans, trimmed
400 g (14 oz) tin butterbeans (lima
  beans), drained and rinsed
85 g (3 oz) mint
70 g (2¹/2 oz/¹/2 cup) pistachios,
  toasted
2 mandarins, zested and juiced
3 tablespoons extra virgin olive oil

Blanch the green beans in boiling salted water for a few minutes, or until they turn a bright emerald green. Drain and rinse the beans under cold running water.

Put the green beans in a salad bowl along with the rinsed butterbeans. Add the mint leaves, pistachio kernels and the grated mandarin zest and toss together. Blend together the mandarin juice and the olive oil in a small bowl. Season with salt and freshly ground black pepper. Dress the salad and serve.

marinated artichokes   serves 4

4 globe artichokes
3 lemons, halved
4 tablespoons olive oil
8 mint leaves, finely chopped
1 handful flat-leaf (Italian) parsley
  leaves, roughly chopped
1 garlic clove, crushed

Bring a large saucepan of salted water to the boil. Fill a bowl with cold water. Add the juice of one of the lemons to it. Trim the artichoke stalks to within 2 cm (3/4 in) of the artichoke head, then pull away the outer leaves until the base of the leaves look yellow and crisp. With a sharp knife, slice away the top third of the artichokes. Rub the artichoke with the cut side of the lemon. Place it in to the water and trim the remaining artichokes.

Remove the artichokes from the water and scrape out the central choke and pull out any of the spiky inner leaves. Return to the water until ready to cook. When the water is boiling, add the artichokes, weigh them down with a plate and simmer for 20 minutes.

Test that the artichokes are done by pushing the tip of a knife into each one just above the stem — it should be tender. Drain the cooked artichokes for a minute then slice in half.

Put in a large dish with the oil, herbs, garlic and juice from the remaining lemon halves. Season with sea salt and freshly ground black pepper.

avocado salsa

1 avocado, finely diced
1 Lebanese (short) cucumber,
   finely diced
1 red chilli, seeded and finely diced
1 tablespoon finely diced red onion
3 tablespoons lime juice
1/2 teaspoon sea salt
1 handful coriander (cilantro) leaves
1 tablespoon extra virgin olive oil

Put the avocado, cucumber, chilli, onion, lime juice and sea salt in a bowl. Add the coriander and olive oil. Lightly stir to combine. Serve with some grilled (broiled) chicken, prawns (shrimp) or white-fleshed fish. This salsa can also be served with warm tortillas or on bruschetta.

baked apples

serves 6

2 tablespoons balsamic vinegar
1 tablespoon honey
20 g (3/4 oz) butter, melted
3 apples, quartered and cored

Preheat the oven to 180°C (350°F/ Gas 4). Put the vinegar in a small bowl with the honey, butter and a generous amount of freshly ground black pepper. Toss the apples in the balsamic marinade. Put them, skin side down, in a small baking tray and drizzle with the remaining marinade. Bake for 30 minutes, then turn the apples over and bake for a further 15 minutes. Serve with roast pork.

sautéed spinach

500 g (1 lb 2 oz) English spinach
20 g (3/4 oz) butter

Rinse the spinach under running water. Remove the stalks and roots and roughly chop the leaves. Heat the butter in a large saucepan over medium heat and add the chopped spinach. Cover with a lid and cook for 2 minutes. Remove from the heat. Season with sea salt and freshly ground black pepper before serving. Serve with poached eggs or chargrilled swordfish.

bean salads

pistachio salad

400 g (14 oz) green beans, blanched
2 tablespoons olive oil
2 tablespoons orange juice
1 teaspoon balsamic vinegar
30 g (1 oz) pistachios, roughly
  chopped

Toss the beans with the olive oil, orange juice, balsamic vinegar and pistachio nuts. Season with sea salt and freshly ground black pepper.

black bean salad

400 g (14 oz) green beans, blanched
2 tablespoons Chinese black beans
30 g (1 oz) almond slivers, lightly
  toasted
1 large red chilli, seeded and
  finely sliced
1 tablespoon lime juice
2 tablespoons olive oil

Toss the beans with the Chinese black beans, almond slivers, chilli, lime juice and olive oil. Season with sea salt and freshly ground black pepper.

minted peas

10 mint leaves
400 g (14 oz) peas
1 tablespoon olive oil

Bring a saucepan of water to the boil. Add the mint, reserving the nicer leaves to fold through the finished dish. When the peas are cooked, drain and then stir in the mint leaves, olive oil and lots of freshly ground pepper.

coconut greens

200 g (7 oz) green beans, trimmed
200 g (7 oz) sugar snap peas, trimmed
1 tablespoon olive oil
2 garlic cloves, crushed
1 tablespoon very finely chopped
   lemon grass, white part only
1 teaspoon paprika
125 ml (4 fl oz/1/2 cup) coconut milk
2 tablespoons fish sauce
1 teaspoon shaved palm sugar
   (jaggery)

Blanch the beans and peas in boiling salted water for 2 minutes, or until they turn bright green. Drain and rinse under running cold water. Set aside.

In a wok or large frying pan, heat the olive oil over medium to high heat and add the garlic, lemon grass and paprika. Stir-fry for 1 minute before adding the coconut milk, 125 ml (4 fl oz/1/2 cup) of water, the fish sauce and palm sugar. Reduce the heat and simmer for 5 minutes, stirring to make sure the sugar dissolves. Add the beans and peas and cook for a further minute. Spoon into a serving bowl. Serve with steamed rice and grilled (broiled) chicken or fish.

nori rolls

rice dressing

4 tablespoons rice vinegar
4 tablespoons sugar
1 tablespoon sea salt

filling ingredients

325 g (11¹/₂ oz/1¹/₂ cups) sushi rice
4 tablespoons pickled ginger
1 teaspoon wasabi
4 nori sheets
2 Lebanese (short) cucumbers, thinly sliced into long lengths
1 avocado, thinly sliced into long lengths
1 daikon, thinly sliced into long lengths

To make the rice dressing, put the rice vinegar into a saucepan with the sugar and sea salt. Heat over medium heat, stirring until the sugar has dissolved. Remove from the heat. Allow to cool.

Cook the sushi rice and then spoon the rice onto a tray. Pour over the rice dressing and allow to cool.

Put the ginger and wasabi into bowls. Lay the first nori sheet onto a sushi mat. Put several spoonfuls of the rice onto the nori sheet. Dip your hands in water and then press out the rice until it covers three-quarters of the nori sheet, leaving one edge clear of rice. Lay the filling ingredients and pickled ginger across the rice.

Dab a little of the wasabi along the edge of the nori sheet where there is no rice. Using the sushi mat, tightly roll the nori and rice, starting from the rice-covered end. Once rolled, set aside and continue with the remaining nori sheets and ingredients. Using a sharp knife, cut the sushi roll into six rounds, approximately 1.5 cm (⁵/₈ in) wide.

chicken and pink grapefruit salad lavash with pastrami fig and goat's cheese salad with a sichuan dressing artichoke, bean and feta salad pea and lettuce soup rocket, pear and parmesan salad warm salad of chestnuts and brussels sprouts grilled haloumi zucchini and sugar snap salad salmon and lime fishcakes potato salad summer salad with toasted pistachio dressing sesame crisps with lime

02 light meals

prawns green chicken salad asparagus with smoked salmon wilted spinach salad squid with chilli dressing chicken and miso soup octopus salad crab and watercress salad prawns with coriander and lime goat's cheese salad with celery pear and parsley

spinach and ricotta omelette

serves 4-6

80 g (2³/4 oz) butter
1 onion, thinly sliced
¹/2 teaspoon ground cumin
pinch of freshly grated nutmeg
500 g (1 lb 2 oz) English spinach,
    washed and trimmed
6 eggs, separated
4 tablespoons roughly chopped flat-leaf
    (Italian) parsley
2 tablespoons finely chopped dill
200 g (7 oz) ricotta cheese
3 tablespoons grated fresh parmesan
    cheese
wholemeal (whole-wheat) toast,
    to serve

Heat a large heavy-based frying pan over a medium heat and add 20 g (³/4 oz) butter, the onion, cumin and nutmeg. Cook until the onion is soft, then add the spinach. Cover and steam for 2 minutes, then remove from the heat and allow to cool. Beat the egg whites in a bowl until they form stiff peaks. Squeeze the spinach of any excess liquid and roughly chop. Combine the spinach and onion mixture in another bowl with the egg yolks, parsley, dill and ricotta. Season with sea salt and freshly ground black pepper, then lightly fold in the egg whites.

Return the pan to high heat and melt the remaining butter. Pour in the egg mixture, then reduce the heat to medium. Cook for 1–2 minutes, then sprinkle with parmesan and place under a grill (broiler) until golden. Serve with wholemeal toast.

lavash with pastrami serves 4

2 red capsicums (peppers)
1 telegraph (long) cucumber
4 pieces lavash or other unleavened
  bread
8 slices pastrami
4 dill pickles, thinly sliced
50 g (1 3/4 oz) baby English spinach

Put the two whole capsicums under a hot grill (broiler) and grill until the skin is beginning to blacken and blister all over. Put the capsicums into a bowl and cover with plastic wrap. When the capsicums have cooled, remove the skin and seeds and thinly slice the flesh. Set aside. Slice the cucumber into long thin strips using a vegetable peeler.

Put one piece of lavash onto a clean dry surface. Put two pieces of pastrami along one side and top with some strips of cucumber, sliced capsicum, dill pickles and spinach leaves. Roll up and set aside. Repeat with the remaining three pieces of bread. Cut the lavash rolls in half and put onto a serving platter.

fig and goat's cheese salad with a sichuan dressing

serves 4

1 teaspoon Sichuan peppercorns,
   crushed
1 teaspoon honey
2 teaspoons balsamic vinegar
3 tablespoons olive oil
1–2 butter lettuces
8 ripe figs, quartered
200 g (7 oz) soft goat's cheese
baguette, to serve

To make the Sichuan dressing, put the peppercorns, honey, vinegar and olive oil into a small bowl and stir until the honey has dissolved. Make the salad by arranging the smallest leaves of the lettuce on four salad plates. Divide the figs between the plates. Crumble the goat's cheese over. Drizzle with the dressing and serve with a baguette.

artichoke, bean and feta salad

4 globe artichokes
2 lemons, halved
4 tablespoons olive oil
8 mint leaves, finely chopped
250 g (9 oz) green beans, trimmed
110 g (3³/4 oz) fresh goat's feta cheese

Bring a saucepan of salted water to the boil. Trim the artichoke stalks to within 2 cm (³/4 in) of the artichoke head, then pull away the outer leaves until the base of the leaves looks yellow and crisp. With a sharp knife, slice away the top third of the artichokes, scrape out the central choke and pull out any of the spiky inner leaves. Rub the artichokes with the cut side of the lemon. When the water is boiling, add the artichokes, weigh them down with a plate and simmer for 20 minutes.

Test that the artichokes are done by pushing the tip of a knife into each one just above the stem — it should be tender. Drain the cooked artichokes upside down for a minute, then slice in half. Put in a large bowl with the olive oil, mint and juice from the remaining lemon halves. Season.

Blanch the beans in boiling water until they turn emerald green, then refresh under cold running water. Divide the artichokes between four plates, pile the beans on top and crumble on the feta. Drizzle with any remaining dressing.

pea and lettuce soup serves 4

2 tablespoons olive oil
1 leek, thinly sliced
1 garlic clove, crushed
1 litre (35 fl oz/4 cups) vegetable
   or chicken stock (basics)
1 butter lettuce, stem removed,
   thinly sliced
125 g (4 1/2 oz/1 cup) fresh peas
1 teaspoon sugar
20 mint leaves
finely grated fresh parmesan cheese,
   to serve

Put the oil, leek and garlic in a large saucepan and sauté until the leek is soft. Add the stock, lettuce and peas and bring to the boil. Reduce the heat and simmer for 15 minutes, or until the peas are soft, then remove the pan from the heat. Add the sugar and mint leaves. Pour the soup mixture into a blender or food processor and whiz until it is smooth. Season well. Serve the soup with some grated parmesan to sprinkle over.

rocket, pear and parmesan salad

serves 4

200 g (7 oz) rocket (arugula)
2 beurre bosc pears, thinly sliced
150 g (5$^1/_2$ oz/1$^1/_2$ cups) shaved
  fresh parmesan cheese
extra virgin olive oil
balsamic vinegar

Put the rocket leaves in a bowl with the pears and parmesan cheese. Drizzle with the extra virgin olive oil and balsamic vinegar and lightly toss.

warm salad of chestnuts and brussels sprouts

serves 4

200 g (7 oz) fresh chestnuts
300 g (10 1/2 oz) brussels sprouts,
   trimmed and cut in half
80 g (2 3/4 oz) butter
1 tablespoon lemon juice
2 tablespoons roughly chopped flat-leaf
   (Italian) parsley

Preheat the oven to 200°C (400°F/ Gas 6). Cut a gash in the outer shell of each of the chestnuts. Put on a baking tray and roast for 15–20 minutes, or until the shells split. Peel the chestnuts while they are still warm and rub off their inner skins. Any particularly stubborn ones can be boiled for a couple of minutes to loosen them. Cut in half if you like.

Bring a saucepan of water to the boil. Tip in the brussels sprouts and cook for 5 minutes. When the sprouts are ready, heat the butter in a frying pan over high heat until it begins to turn a golden brown colour. Add the lemon juice, chestnuts and brussels sprouts to the pan and toss together. Season to taste. Scatter over the chopped parsley and serve.

fried haloumi

serves 4

250 g (9 oz) haloumi cheese
2 Lebanese (short) cucumbers
1/2 red onion, thinly sliced
3 handfuls mint
1 tablespoon lemon juice
185 ml (6 fl oz/3/4 cup) olive oil

Slice the haloumi lengthways into eight thick slices. Trim the ends from the cucumbers, cut in half and then again lengthways into long thin strips. Put the cucumber in a bowl along with the onion, mint leaves, lemon juice and 125 ml (4 fl oz/1/2 cup) of olive oil. Toss together. Season with salt and pepper and divide the salad between four plates.

Heat the remaining olive oil in a frying pan over high heat. Fry each of the haloumi pieces on both sides. Put the cheese on top of the salad and serve immediately.

zucchini and sugar snap salad

200 g (7 oz) sugar snap peas, trimmed
4 zucchini (courgettes), trimmed and
    thickly sliced
6–8 radishes, trimmed and thinly sliced
1 tablespoon lemon juice
3 tablespoons walnut oil
1 teaspoon celery salt
2 tablespoons pepitas (pumpkin
    seeds), toasted

Bring a pot of salted water to the boil. Add the sugar snap peas and blanch until they are bright green. Remove with a slotted spoon and rinse under running cold water. Add the zucchini to the boiling water and cook for 2 minutes. Put the zucchini and sugar snap peas in a bowl with the radishes. To make the dressing, put the lemon juice, walnut oil, celery salt and some freshly ground black pepper into a small bowl and stir to combine. Drizzle the dressing over the salad. Scatter the toasted pepitas over the top.

salmon and lime fishcakes

serves 4

6 makrut (kaffir lime) leaves, 2 very finely sliced and chopped

500 g (1 lb 2 oz) salmon fillet, boned and skin removed

160 g (5¾ oz/2 cups) fresh breadcrumbs

2 tablespoons finely chopped coriander (cilantro) leaves

2 tablespoons very finely chopped lemon grass, white part only

2 large red chillies, seeded and finely chopped

30 g (1 oz/½ cup) thinly sliced spring onions (scallions)

2 eggs

1 teaspoon fish sauce

1 tablespoon lime juice

½ teaspoon ground white pepper

4 tablespoons vegetable oil

2 limes, halved, to serve

green salad, to serve

Put 250 ml (9 fl oz/1 cup) of water and 4 makrut leaves in a frying pan over high heat. Add the salmon, then reduce the heat and simmer, covered, for 5 minutes, or until cooked through. Remove the salmon from the pan and allow to cool.

Using a fork, break up the cooled salmon and combine in a bowl with the breadcrumbs, sliced makrut leaves, coriander, lemon grass, chillies, spring onions, eggs, fish sauce, lime juice and white pepper. Shape into 12 patties. Heat some oil in a non-stick frying pan over medium heat. Cook the fishcakes, in batches, until they are golden brown. Add oil to the pan as you need it. Serve with lime halves and a green salad.

potato salad

4 large desiree or pontiac potatoes
6 spring onions (scallions), thinly sliced
75 g (2¹/₂ oz) flat-leaf (Italian) parsley,
   roughly chopped
70 g (2¹/₂ oz) dill, finely chopped
125 ml (4 fl oz/¹/₂ cup) olive oil
1 lemon, zested and juiced

Cut the potatoes into chunks. Put in a large saucepan of salted cold water and bring to the boil over high heat. When the water has reached boiling point, cover the pan with a lid and remove it from the heat. Leave the potatoes to sit for half an hour. (This is a nice way to cook the potatoes because they don't break up or become waterlogged.)

Meanwhile, mix the spring onions, parsley, dill, olive oil, lemon zest and juice together. When the potatoes are ready, test them with the point of a sharp knife — they should be tender and cooked through. Drain and add to the herbed dressing while they are still hot. Toss to combine and season with salt and freshly ground black pepper.

summer salad with toasted pistachio dressing serves 4

2 Lebanese (short) cucumbers,
   thinly sliced
90 g (3¼ oz/1 cup) bean sprouts,
   trimmed
1 red capsicum (pepper), julienned
1 orange, segments removed and
   thinly sliced in half lengthways
30 g (1 oz) chives, chopped into 2 cm
   (¾ in) lengths
2 handfuls baby rocket (arugula) leaves
1 teaspoon finely grated fresh ginger
1 teaspoon honey
2 tablespoons lemon juice
1 teaspoon wasabi paste
4 tablespoons olive oil
130 g (4¾ oz) pistachios, toasted
   and roughly chopped

Put the cucumbers, bean sprouts, capsicum, orange, chives and rocket into a large serving bowl and toss to combine.

To make the toasted pistachio dressing, put the ginger, honey, lemon juice, wasabi and olive oil in a small bowl. Stir well to combine. Season with a little sea salt and freshly ground black pepper. Add the pistachios then pour over the salad.

sesame crisps with lime prawns

1 tablespoon finely chopped lemon
  grass, white part only
1 red chilli, seeded and finely chopped
2 tablespoons lime juice
3 tablespoons olive oil
16 large raw prawns (shrimp), peeled
  and deveined with tails intact
80 g (2³/4 oz) coriander (cilantro) sprigs
90 g (3¹/4 oz/¹/3 cup) lemon
  mayonnaise (basics)

sesame crisps

1 egg
80 g (2³/4 oz/¹/2 cup) sesame seeds
250 ml (9 fl oz/1 cup) peanut oil
8 wonton wrappers

Put the lemon grass, chilli, lime juice and olive oil in a bowl. Add the prawns to the bowl. Cover and place in the fridge for several hours.

To make the sesame crisps, whisk the egg and 1 tablespoon of water in a small bowl. Put the sesame seeds in another small bowl. Heat the oil in a deep frying pan or wok over high heat. Brush the egg wash onto one of the wrappers, then sprinkle with the sesame seeds. When the oil is hot, add the wonton and fry for 30 seconds, or until it is puffed and golden brown. Remove the wrapper from the pan. Drain on paper towels. Repeat with the remaining wrappers.

Heat a large non-stick frying pan over medium heat. Add the prawns and cook for 2–3 minutes, or until they are pink and beginning to curl up.

To assemble, place a sesame crisp on each serving plate. Top with the prawns, coriander sprigs, a large dollop of lemon mayonnaise and the remaining sesame crisps.

green chicken salad   serves 4

2 skinless, boneless chicken breasts
   (400 g/14 oz), poached and shredded
3 spring onions (scallions), thinly sliced
   on the diagonal
1 large handful roughly chopped
   coriander (cilantro) leaves
1 large handful roughly chopped mint
20 g (3/4 oz/1/4 cup) dried Asian fried
   onions
2 tablespoons sesame seeds, toasted
2 tablespoons lime juice
2 tablespoons fish sauce
2 teaspoons grated fresh ginger
2 red chillies, seeded and finely
   chopped
1 tablespoon shaved palm sugar
   (jaggery)

Place the shredded chicken meat, spring onions, coriander, mint leaves, fried onions and sesame seeds in a large bowl and mix together. In a small bowl, mix together the lime juice, fish sauce, ginger, chillies and palm sugar. Stir until the sugar has dissolved, then pour over the salad.

asparagus with smoked salmon

serves 4

1 egg yolk
1 teaspoon Dijon mustard
1 tablespoon lemon juice
1/2 teaspoon sugar
125 ml (4 fl oz/1/2 cup) light olive oil
350 g (12 oz) asparagus, ends trimmed
30 g (1 oz/1 cup) croutons
200 g (7 oz) watercress, stalks
  removed
8 slices smoked salmon

Whisk together the egg yolk, mustard, lemon juice, sugar and a pinch of salt. Slowly add the olive oil, whisking until the mixture becomes thick and creamy. Set aside.

Bring a saucepan of water to the boil. Cook the asparagus for 4 minutes, or until it is tender. Refresh under cold running water. Drain the asparagus well. Put the dressing, asparagus, croutons and watercress in a large bowl and toss together. Divide the salmon between four plates. Top with a pile of the salad. Season with freshly ground black pepper.

wilted spinach salad   serves 4

1 kg (2 lb 4 oz) English spinach, rinsed
  and stalks removed
12 kalamata olives, pitted and roughly
  chopped
1 garlic clove, finely chopped
2 tablespoons finely chopped mint
1 small red onion, halved and thinly
  sliced
2 tablespoons red wine vinegar
200 g (7 oz) feta cheese, crumbled
125 ml (4 fl oz/1/2 cup) olive oil
30 g (1 oz/1 cup) croutons

Make sure the spinach is well drained before roughly chopping the larger leaves and placing in a large metal bowl. Add the olives, garlic, mint, onion and vinegar then crumble the feta cheese over. Heat the olive oil in a frying pan over high heat until it is almost smoking, then pour it over the salad. Be careful to stand well back as some of the oil may splatter. Toss the ingredients one more time and pile into a serving bowl. Scatter with croutons and serve immediately.

squid with chilli dressing

serves 4

1 small red chilli, seeded and finely chopped
4 tablespoons rice wine vinegar
2 tablespoons extra virgin olive oil
1 teaspoon sesame oil
2 teaspoons caster (superfine) sugar
2 teaspoons fish sauce
1 tablespoon lime juice
1 tablespoon finely chopped mint
400 g (14 oz) watercress, stalks removed
130 g (4³/4 oz) daikon radish, julienned
600 g (1 lb 5 oz) baby squid, cleaned

To make the chilli dressing, put the chilli, rice wine vinegar, olive oil, sesame oil, sugar, fish sauce, lime juice and mint in a bowl and stir to combine. Toss the watercress sprigs and the daikon together in a bowl. Pile onto four small plates.

Score the surface of the squid tubes in a crisscross pattern with a sharp knife. Heat a non-stick frying pan over a high heat. Cook the squid for 1–2 minutes, or until it is just white. Remove from the heat and slice into thick bite-sized pieces. Put into the bowl with the chilli dressing and toss until the squid is well coated. Place the squid pieces onto the salad and spoon over the remaining dressing.

chicken and miso soup serves 4

6 dried shiitake mushrooms
1 litre (35 fl oz/4 cups) chicken stock
(basics)
3 cm (1¼ in) piece fresh ginger, peeled
and cut into thick rounds
1 small cinnamon stick
2 x 200 g (7 oz) skinless, boneless
chicken breast fillets, finely sliced
on the diagonal
6 spring onions (scallions), trimmed
and cut into 2 cm (¼ in) lengths
8 baby corn, cut in half lengthways
2 tablespoons white miso
100 g (3½ oz) sugar snap peas,
trimmed

Put the mushrooms in a bowl and cover with 250 ml (9 fl oz/1 cup) of hot water. Allow to soak for 10 minutes. Remove the mushrooms and strain the liquid into a large saucepan. Discard the tough stems of the mushrooms and thinly slice the caps. Add them to the saucepan along with the stock, ginger and cinnamon. Bring to the boil then reduce to a simmer. Simmer for 10 minutes, remove the cinnamon and add the chicken, spring onions and baby corn. Simmer for a further 5 minutes before adding the miso and peas. Heat the soup until nearly boiling. Ladle into four bowls.

octopus salad

6–8 small desiree or pontiac potatoes
1 teaspoon sea salt
2 lemons, juiced
4 garlic cloves
10–12 sprigs thyme
8 small baby octopus, cleaned
2 handfuls baby rocket (arugula) leaves
2 handfuls flat-leaf (Italian) parsley
60 g (2¼ oz/⅓ cup) small black olives
3 tablespoons extra virgin olive oil
1 lemon, cut into wedges

Put the potatoes in a large pot and fill with cold water. Add the sea salt, lemon juice, garlic and thyme. Bring to the boil and cook for 10 minutes. Add the octopus and continue to cook for another 10 minutes. Remove from the heat and allow the octopus and potatoes to cool in the water. When cool, remove the potatoes and octopus and cut them into bite-sized chunks.

Divide the rocket and most of the parsley between four plates. Arrange the potatoes and octopus over the leaves. Scatter with the olives and garnish with the remaining parsley. Lightly season with sea salt and freshly ground black pepper. Drizzle with the olive oil. Serve with lemon wedges.

marinated bocconcini salad

serves 4

3 tablespoons extra virgin olive oil
1 handful flat-leaf (Italian) parsley
1 tablespoon thyme
10 mint leaves, roughly torn
2 tablespoons finely chopped chives
10 basil leaves, roughly torn
4 bocconcini (fresh baby mozzarella cheese), cut into quarters
24 small black olives
2 tablespoons balsamic vinegar

Put the olive oil, parsley, thyme, mint, chives and basil in a bowl. Add the bocconcini and toss until it is well coated. Season with sea salt and freshly ground black pepper. Set aside for 1 hour or overnight to marinate.

Pile the marinated cheese into a serving bowl. Scatter with the olives. Drizzle with balsamic vinegar and season to taste.

crab and watercress salad

serves 4

100 ml (3½ fl oz) tamarind water
  (basics)
2 tablespoons shaved palm sugar
  (jaggery)
2 tablespoons fish sauce
2 tablespoons lime juice
250 g (9 oz) fresh cooked crab meat
2 tablespoons light olive oil
2 tablespoons finely chopped
  coriander (cilantro) leaves
400 g (14 oz) watercress, stalks
  removed
1 yellow capsicum (pepper), julienned
3 large red chillies, seeded and thinly
  sliced
2 spring onions (scallions), thinly sliced

To make the dressing, put the tamarind water, palm sugar, fish sauce and lime juice in a small bowl and stir until the sugar has dissolved. Set aside.

Put the crab meat into another bowl and break up the meat into fine threads. Add the olive oil and coriander and stir until well combined. Season with sea salt and freshly ground black pepper. Mix the watercress, capsicum, chillies and spring onions in a large bowl. Drizzle with the dressing and toss until all the ingredients are well coated. Divide between four plates and top with a large spoonful of the crab meat.

prawns with coriander and lime

serves 4

2 tablespoons chopped coriander
  (cilantro) root
2 tablespoons grated fresh ginger
2 garlic cloves, roughly chopped
1 lemon grass stem, white part only,
  roughly chopped
125 ml (4 fl oz/1/2 cup) vegetable oil
1 teaspoon ground coriander
20 large raw prawns (shrimp), peeled
  and deveined with tails intact
30 g (1 oz) coriander (cilantro) leaves
60 ml (2 fl oz/1/4 cup) lime juice
125 ml (4 fl oz/1/2 cup) olive oil
1/2 teaspoon sugar
20 small bamboo skewers, soaked in
  hot water for 20 minutes

Place the coriander root, ginger, garlic, lemon grass, vegetable oil and ground coriander in a blender and blend to form a smooth paste. Place the prawns in a ceramic or glass dish and pour over the paste. Allow to marinate, covered in the refrigerator, for at least 1 hour.

Blend the coriander leaves, lime juice, olive oil, sugar and a pinch of salt together and set aside. Place a prawn on each of the bamboo skewers. Grill on a moderately hot preheated barbecue for 5 minutes. Serve with a drizzle of the coriander dressing.

goat's cheese salad with celery, pear and parsley

serves 4

1 tablespoon white wine vinegar
3 tablespoons extra virgin olive oil
3 celery stalks, thinly sliced
3 nashi pears, thinly sliced
1 handful flat-leaf (Italian) parsley
25 g (1 oz/¼ cup) flaked almonds, toasted
150 g (5½ oz) fresh goat's cheese

Put the vinegar and extra virgin olive oil in a large bowl. Season with sea salt and freshly ground black pepper. Stir to combine, then add the celery, pear, parsley and almonds. Toss, then pile onto a serving platter. Crumble the goat's cheese over the salad and serve immediately.

capsicum salad with tuna and egg

serves 4

1 garlic clove, crushed

1 1/2 tablespoons red wine vinegar

3 tablespoons olive oil

1 green capsicum (pepper), finely diced

1 yellow capsicum (pepper), finely diced

3 ripe tomatoes, cut into wedges

150 g (5 1/2 oz) baby rocket (arugula) leaves

185 g (6 1/2 oz) tinned tuna, drained

4 hard-boiled eggs, quartered

5 handfuls flat-leaf (Italian) parsley, roughly chopped

Mix the garlic, vinegar, olive oil, diced capsicum and tomatoes together in a bowl. Pile four plates with baby rocket and top with the capsicum salad, tuna, boiled eggs and parsley. Season with salt and pepper.

smoked trout fishcakes with wilted spinach   serves 4

2 potatoes, peeled
2 spring onions (scallions), thinly sliced
200 g (7 oz) smoked trout, boned and
    skin removed
75 g (2¹/₂ oz) dill, finely chopped
2 tablespoons finely chopped chives
1 egg
60 ml (2 fl oz/¹/₄ cup) oil
40 g (1¹/₂ oz) butter
750 g (1 lb 10 oz) English spinach,
    stalks removed
lemon halves, to serve

Cut the potatoes into chunks. Put in a saucepan of salted cold water. Bring to the boil and cook at a simmer until tender. Drain and mash the potatoes. Add the spring onions, smoked trout, dill and chives to the mash and mix together. Season and stir in the egg. Form the mixture into 16 patties.

Heat the oil in a frying pan and cook the patties in batches until they are golden brown and crisp on both sides. Drain on paper towels.

Heat the butter in another pan and sauté the spinach for about a minute, so that it is just wilted. Pile the spinach onto four plates. Add the fishcakes. Serve with lemon halves.

chicken and papaya salad

serves 4

2 boneless roast chicken breasts,
   roughly shredded
80 g (2³/₄ oz/¹/₂ cup) peanuts, roughly
   chopped
1 orange papaya, peeled, seeded
   and sliced
1 Lebanese (short) cucumber, diced
2 tablespoons dried Asian fried onions
2 spring onions (scallions), shredded
3 handfuls mint
15 betel leaves

dressing
125 ml (4 fl oz/¹/₂ cup) tamarind water
   (basics)
1 teaspoon soy sauce
2 teaspoons finely grated fresh ginger
1 tablespoon shaved palm sugar
   (jaggery)
¹/₂ teaspoon ground cumin
1 large red chilli, seeded and thinly
   sliced

To make the dressing, mix the
tamarind water, soy sauce, ginger,
palm sugar, cumin and chilli together
in a bowl. Keep stirring until the sugar
has dissolved.

Add the chicken to the dressing and
toss. Combine the remaining salad
ingredients, except the betel leaves, in
another bowl. Season with salt and
freshly ground black pepper.

Arrange the betel leaves on four plates
and top with the salad, chicken and
any remaining dressing.

field mushrooms on puff pastry

serves 4

4 field mushrooms
2 tablespoons olive oil
1 garlic clove, crushed
1 sheet butter puff pastry
120 g (4¼ oz) rocket (arugula)
70 g (2½ oz) shaved fresh parmesan cheese
1 tablespoon balsamic vinegar

Preheat the oven to 180°C (350°F/ Gas 4). Remove the stem from each of the mushrooms and put the caps into a large bowl with the olive oil, garlic and some sea salt and freshly ground black pepper. Coat the mushrooms in the garlicky oil.

Cut the butter puff into four squares and lay them on a baking tray. Roll the edges of each square over to form a raised edge, then put a mushroom into the centre of each pastry square. Bake for 20 minutes, or until the pastry is puffed and golden.

Tear the rocket leaves into bite-sized pieces, then toss with the parmesan and vinegar. Season to taste. Pile the rocket salad on top of the mushroom tartlets. Serve while still warm.

chicken and pink grapefruit salad

serves 4

1 spring onion (scallion), thinly sliced
2 tablespoons white wine vinegar
4 tablespoons extra virgin olive oil
90 g (3¼ oz/⅓ cup) crème fraîche
175 g (6 oz) roast chicken meat, shredded
2 pink grapefruits
3 handfuls mixed mizuna, lamb's lettuce (corn salad) and English spinach leaves
8 walnuts, chopped

Put the sliced spring onion, vinegar, olive oil and crème fraîche in a bowl and stir to combine. If too thick, add a little warm water. Add the shredded chicken meat and toss so as to coat the chicken pieces all over. Using a sharp knife, peel the grapefruits and remove the segments by slicing between each of the membranes.

Arrange a bed of mixed salad leaves on the serving plate. Top with the chicken. Scatter the grapefruit and walnuts over the top of the salad. Season with a little sea salt and freshly ground black pepper.

octopus with thai dressing

serves 4

2 red chillies, seeded and finely
  chopped
1 garlic clove, crushed
1 tablespoon shaved palm sugar
  (jaggery)
1 tablespoon lime juice
3 tablespoons fish sauce
1 tablespoon rice wine vinegar
3 tablespoons olive oil
2 tablespoons white wine vinegar
1 tablespoon finely chopped coriander
  (cilantro)
16 small octopus, cleaned
baby leaf salad, to serve
lime wedges, to serve

To make the Thai dressing, combine the chillies, garlic, palm sugar, lime juice, fish sauce and rice wine vinegar with 3 tablespoons of water and stir until the sugar has dissolved.

Mix the olive oil, vinegar and coriander together in a bowl and add the octopus. Cover and leave to marinate for a few hours, or preferably overnight in the fridge.

Remove the octopus from the marinade and grill it on a hot barbecue or grill plate for a few minutes on each side until it looks charred around the edges and is cooked through. Serve the octopus on a baby leaf salad with the Thai dressing and lime wedges.

chicken and preserved
lemon salad

1 tablespoon sea salt

2 lemons, juiced

2 skinless, boneless chicken breasts

3 tablespoons olive oil

1 teaspoon ground cumin

1 tablespoon finely chopped preserved
lemon

90 g (3¼ oz/1 cup) almond flakes,
toasted

50 g (1¾ oz) roughly chopped
coriander (cilantro)

5 handfuls mint, roughly chopped

60 g (2¼ oz/½ cup) sultanas (golden
raisins)

Bring a saucepan of water to the boil, add the salt, half the lemon juice and the chicken breasts, bring back to the boil, cover and remove from the heat. Leave the saucepan to sit for half an hour. Remove the chicken breasts from the water, drain well and thinly slice against the grain.

Put the chicken in a large bowl and add the olive oil, ground cumin, preserved lemon, the rest of the lemon juice and the almond flakes. Toss together, then add the remaining ingredients and toss again.

caesar salad

1 teaspoon Dijon mustard
2 tablespoons lemon juice
3 eggs
205 ml (7 fl oz) olive oil
3 tablespoons grated fresh parmesan
cheese
2 rashers of bacon, thinly sliced
3 slices sourdough bread, crusts
removed, chopped
2 cos (romaine) lettuces
4 anchovies, finely chopped

Whisk together the mustard, lemon juice and 1 egg. Add 125 ml (4 fl oz/ 1/2 cup) olive oil, whisking constantly. Stir through the parmesan cheese and season with sea salt and freshly ground black pepper. Boil the remaining eggs for 6 minutes. Heat the remaining olive oil in a frying pan and fry the bacon over medium heat. As the bacon cooks, remove and drain on paper towels. Add the bread to the oil and fry until golden brown. Roughly chop the hearts of the cos lettuces and put on a serving platter. Shell and quarter the eggs. Add the eggs, bacon, fried bread and the anchovies to the platter. Drizzle with the dressing.

white bean and herb soup

serves 4

2 tablespoons olive oil
2 onions, finely diced
200 g (7 oz) celery, thinly sliced
1 litre (35 fl oz/4 cups) vegetable or
 chicken stock (basics)
400 g (14 oz/1¹/2 cups) cooked white
 beans, such as cannellini
45 g (1¹/2 oz) roughly chopped flat-leaf
 (Italian) parsley
10 basil leaves, finely chopped
125 g (4¹/2 oz/¹/2 cup) light sour cream
10 mint leaves, finely chopped
crusty bread, to serve

Heat the oil in a large saucepan over a medium heat. Add the onions and celery and sauté until the onions are soft and transparent. Mix in the stock and white beans and simmer for 30 minutes.

Just before serving, add the parsley and basil. Cook for a further minute and then ladle the soup into four soup bowls. Add the sour cream, garnish with the chopped mint and serve with thick slices of crusty bread.

salmon carpaccio

1 small fennel bulb, trimmed
1/2 teaspoon sea salt
1 teaspoon finely chopped mint
1 teaspoon finely chopped dill
1 teaspoon sugar
1 lemon, juiced
310 g (11 oz) sashimi salmon, boned
   and skin removed
small salted capers, rinsed and
   drained, to serve
extra virgin olive oil, for drizzling

Cut the fennel bulb into paper-thin slices and finely chop the feathery fennel tops. Put the sliced fennel and fennel tops in a bowl along with the sea salt, chopped herbs, sugar and lemon juice and toss everything together. Cover the salad and put it in the fridge for at least an hour.

Check that all the bones have been removed from the salmon fillet before wrapping it in plastic wrap and putting it in the freezer for half an hour to firm it up. Cut the chilled salmon into paper-thin strips with a sharp knife.

Divide the salmon slices between four small plates. Top with the fennel salad, arranging it so that the salmon slices can be seen through the fennel. Sprinkle with the capers and drizzle with extra virgin olive oil.

pear and walnut salad

100 g (3¹/2 oz/1 cup) walnut halves
¹/2 garlic clove
1 orange, zest grated, juiced
1 teaspoon sea salt
125 ml (4 fl oz/¹/2 cup) light olive oil
240 g (8¹/2 oz) rocket (arugula)
2 beurre bosc pears
140 g (5 oz) goat's curd

Put the walnuts, garlic, grated orange zest, sea salt and olive oil in a blender or food processor and whiz to form a sauce. Toss the rocket leaves in the orange juice and divide the leaves between four plates.

Core the pears, slice them thinly and arrange the slices over the rocket. Top with the goat's curd, pour the walnut dressing over the salad and season.

green papaya salad

serves 4

3 tablespoons lime juice
3 tablespoons fish sauce
3 tablespoons sugar
2 large red chillies, seeded and
  finely chopped
1 tablespoon finely chopped mint
1 green papaya
2 tablespoons roasted peanuts,
  finely chopped
1 large handful coriander (cilantro)
  leaves

To make the dressing, put the lime juice, fish sauce, sugar, chilli and mint in a bowl and stir until the sugar has dissolved.

Peel the papaya and cut the flesh into pieces. Finely julienne or grate the papaya and add it to the dressing along with the peanuts and coriander. Toss the salad ingredients together and serve immediately.

green bean salad with cherry tomatoes and haloumi

serves 4

150 g (5 1/2 oz) green beans, trimmed
200 g (7 oz) flat green beans, trimmed
1 tablespoon lemon juice
2 tablespoons extra virgin olive oil
250 g (9 oz) cherry tomatoes, cut
   into quarters
1 handful mint
1 handful basil
250 g (9 oz) haloumi cheese
1 tablespoon olive oil

Slice the green beans into halves and the flat beans into 1 cm (1/2 in) lengths. Put the lemon juice and extra virgin olive oil in a large bowl and season with a little sea salt and freshly ground black pepper. Bring a pot of salted water to the boil. Add the beans and cook until they are bright green. Drain and toss the beans in the lemon juice and olive oil. When the beans are cool, add the cherry tomatoes, mint and basil.

Cut the haloumi into eight slices. Heat the olive oil in a frying pan over high heat and fry the haloumi pieces on both sides until golden brown. Put a haloumi slice on each serving plates. Spoon the bean salad over then top with the remaining pieces of haloumi.

watercress and duck salad

serves 4

125 ml (4 fl oz/1/2 cup) sherry
125 ml (4 fl oz/1/2 cup) orange juice
1 tablespoon soy sauce
1 teaspoon sesame oil
1 teaspoon sugar
1 teaspoon finely grated fresh ginger
1 Chinese roast duck
110 g (3³/4 oz) snow peas (mangetout),
  trimmed
400 g (14 oz) watercress, stalks
  removed
200 g (7 oz) tin water chestnuts,
  drained and sliced

To make the dressing, put the sherry and orange juice in a small saucepan. Bring to the boil, then reduce the heat and allow to simmer until the liquid has reduced by half. Pour into a bowl and add the soy sauce, sesame oil, sugar and ginger.

Remove the skin from the roast duck and cut it into thin strips, scraping off any fat. Lay the skin strips on a tray and grill (broil) briefly until they crisp up, then put on a paper towel to drain off any fat.

Remove the meat from the roast duck and tear it into strips before adding it to the bowl of dressing. Blanch the snow peas in boiling water and refresh under cold running water.

Toss the duck meat with the water chestnuts, watercress, snow peas and crisp skin and serve.

coconut and green bean salad

400 g (14 oz) green beans, trimmed
2 green chillies, finely chopped
1 teaspoon grated fresh ginger
90 g (3¼ oz/⅓ cup) plain yoghurt
1 lime, juiced
1 teaspoon sea salt
¼ coconut, flesh freshly shaved
2 tablespoons vegetable oil
1 tablespoon brown mustard seeds
30 curry leaves

Bring a saucepan of water to the boil and cook the green beans for 2–3 minutes until they are brilliant green. Drain and refresh the beans under cold running water.

Put the chillies, ginger, yoghurt, lime juice and sea salt in a bowl, add the coconut and toss everything together. Heat the oil over medium heat in a small frying pan, add the mustard seeds and curry leaves, and when the seeds begin to pop take the pan off the heat. Add the seeds and leaves to the coconut mixture with the green beans and toss together.

sesame salad

4 tablespoons olive oil
1 tablespoon soy sauce
1 teaspoon sesame oil
2 tablespoons lime juice
1 teaspoon sugar
1 teaspoon finely grated fresh ginger
20 snow peas (mangetout), trimmed
140 g (5 oz) oyster mushrooms,
    quartered
5 handfuls coriander (cilantro) leaves
1 red capsicum (pepper), julienned
2 spring onions (scallions), trimmed
    and thinly sliced
1 large red chilli, seeded and finely
    chopped
3 tablespoons sesame seeds

To make the dressing, combine the olive oil, soy sauce, sesame oil, lime juice, sugar and ginger in a small bowl. Blanch the snow peas in boiling water and refresh under cold running water. Slice the peas in half lengthways and put in a bowl with the oyster mushrooms, coriander leaves, red capsicum, spring onions and chilli. Add the dressing and toss together. Season to taste.

Heat a non-stick frying pan over high heat, add the sesame seeds and lightly stir until they are beginning to brown. Sprinkle the seeds over the salad.

squid and pine nut salad

serves 4

450 g (1 lb) small squid
4 anchovy fillets, finely chopped
2 tablespoons olive oil
1 lemon, zested and juiced
2 garlic cloves, crushed
150 g (5^1/$_2$ oz) rocket (arugula)
3 handfuls flat-leaf (Italian) parsley
50 g (1^3/$_4$ oz) shaved fresh parmesan cheese
80 g (2^3/$_4$ oz/^{1}/$_2$ cup) pine nuts, toasted

Combine the squid, anchovy fillets, olive oil, lemon zest and garlic in a bowl and toss well to coat the squid thoroughly. Cover the squid and allow it to marinate for at least an hour.

Put a heavy-based frying pan over high heat. Cook the squid, searing it on both sides for 1–2 minutes. Pour on the marinade and cook for a further 30 seconds. Turn off the heat and allow the squid to sit for a few minutes before slicing it into thin rings. Put the squid in a bowl along with the remaining ingredients, except the lemon juice. Dress with the lemon juice and toss together.

salad of roast potatoes and smoked trout

serves 4

4 large potatoes, cut into wedges
1 lemon, zested and juiced
125 ml (4 fl oz/1/2 cup) light olive oil
2 tablespoons finely chopped dill
400 g (14 oz) hot smoked ocean trout,
    broken into pieces
100 g (3 1/2 oz) baby English spinach
1 large handful flat-leaf (Italian) parsley,
    roughly chopped

Preheat the oven to 180°C (350°F/ Gas 4). Put the potatoes in a baking dish with 250 ml (9 fl oz/1 cup) of water. Season generously with sea salt and add the lemon zest and 4 tablespoons of the oil. Bake for 20 minutes.

Whisk the lemon juice with the remaining oil and the dill. Season to taste.

Turn the potatoes over and cook for a further 20 minutes. When the potatoes are golden brown, divide between four bowls. Top with the ocean trout, spinach leaves and a scattering of parsley. Spoon the dill dressing over the salad before serving.

white chicken salad serves 4

4 spring onions (scallions), thinly
   sliced, green tops reserved
1 lemon grass stem, bruised
80 g (2³/4 oz) coriander (cilantro)
1 tablespoon sea salt
2 skinless, boneless chicken breasts
400 g (14 oz/2 cups) jasmine rice
90 g (3¹/4 oz) mint
1 large red chilli, seeded and finely
   chopped
300 g (10¹/2 oz) silken firm tofu, cut
   into 4 thick slices
soy sauce, to serve
lime wedges, to serve

Put the green tops of the spring onions into a large saucepan with the lemon grass and coriander roots and stalks. Fill the pan with water, add the salt and bring to the boil. Drop the chicken into the liquid, cover the pan and remove from the heat. Leave it covered for 40 minutes. Lift the chicken out of the stock and check that they are cooked. Thinly slice the chicken across the grain. Reserve the liquid.

Put the rice and 685 ml (23¹/2 fl oz/ 2³/4 cups) of the strained cooking liquid in a saucepan. Bring to the boil. Cover and cook for 25 minutes, or until the liquid has been absorbed and the rice is tender. Thinly slice half the mint leaves. Stir the spring onions, sliced mint, coriander leaves, chilli and chicken into the rice. Divide between four bowls and top with a slice of tofu. Splash the tofu with some soy, and serve with a lime wedge and the whole mint leaves.

green tea noodles with lemon grass and soy

serves 4

2 lemon grass stems, white part only, finely chopped
1 tablespoon finely grated fresh ginger
3¹/₂ tablespoons soy sauce
3¹/₂ tablespoons sesame oil
1¹/₂ tablespoons balsamic vinegar
2 tablespoons sugar
1 lemon, juiced
300 g (10¹/₂ oz) dried green tea noodles
2 spring onions (scallions), thinly sliced
90 g (3¹/₄ oz) coriander (cilantro) leaves
1 red capsicum (pepper), finely diced
1 yellow capsicum (pepper), finely diced

Put the lemon grass, ginger, soy sauce, sesame oil, balsamic vinegar, sugar and lemon juice in a small bowl. Stir until the sugar has dissolved. Set aside.

Bring a large pot of water to the boil and add the noodles. Cook for 4–5 minutes, or until *al dente*. Drain well and transfer the noodles to a large bowl. Drizzle with the dressing, lightly tossing the noodles to ensure they are all coated. Add the sliced spring onions, coriander leaves and diced capsicum. Toss again before dividing among four bowls. Serve as a light meal, or alongside some grilled (broiled) prawns (shrimp), fish or chicken.

chicken and coconut soup

1 teaspoon sesame oil
1 red chilli, seeded and thinly sliced
2 skinless, boneless chicken breasts,
  thinly sliced across the grain
4 spring onions (scallions), trimmed
  and sliced on the diagonal
1 red capsicum (pepper), thinly sliced
1.5 litres (52 fl oz/6 cups) chicken
  stock (basics)
400 ml (14 fl oz) coconut milk
3 tablespoons lime juice
1 tablespoon fish sauce
2 large handfuls coriander (cilantro)
  leaves, chopped
100 g (3 1/2 oz) snow pea (mangetout)
  shoots, cut into short lengths
lime wedges, to serve

Put the sesame oil, chilli and chicken in a wok or saucepan over medium heat and stir-fry until the chicken is beginning to brown. Add the spring onions, capsicum, chicken stock, coconut milk, lime juice and fish sauce. Bring to the boil and simmer for 10 minutes.

At the last minute, throw in the coriander and snow pea shoots. Season to taste with salt and pepper. Serve immediately with lime wedges to squeeze over.

smoked trout and cucumber salad

serves 4

2 telegraph (long) cucumbers, peeled
   and seeded
1 tablespoon sea salt
1 smoked rainbow trout (about 250 g/
   9 oz)
1 teaspoon sugar
1 tablespoon lemon juice
30 g (1 oz) chives, finely chopped
125 ml (4 fl oz/1/2 cup) cream
   (whipping)
1 tablespoon finely chopped dill
400 g (14 oz) watercress, broken
   into sprigs

Thinly slice the cucumbers, sprinkle with the sea salt and leave to drain in a colander for 30 minutes.

Take the skin off the trout and flake the flesh, making sure that you remove all the small bones. Squeeze any liquid from the cucumber slices and put in a large bowl along with the smoked trout. Blend together the sugar, lemon juice, chives, cream and fresh dill. Pour the dressing over the cucumber and trout and toss to combine. Divide the watercress leaves between four plates. Top with the cucumber and trout salad.

warm salad of avocado and prosciutto

serves 4

1 teaspoon thyme
1/2 teaspoon soft brown sugar
1 teaspoon Dijon mustard
3 tablespoons extra virgin olive oil
1 tablespoon balsamic vinegar
2 avocados, thickly sliced
2 Lebanese (short) cucumbers,
   thinly sliced
2 tablespoons pine nuts, toasted
120 g (4 1/4 oz) mesclun salad mix
6 slices prosciutto

To make the dressing, blend the thyme, brown sugar, mustard, oil and vinegar together in a small bowl. Arrange the avocados, cucumbers and pine nuts on top of the mesclun. Slice the prosciutto into 4 cm (1 1/2 in) pieces and grill (broil) or fry until it is crisp and golden. Tip the hot prosciutto into the salad dressing and toss together before pouring it over the salad.

polenta pancakes with spinach and smoked salmon

serves 4

250 ml (9 fl oz/1 cup) milk
2 lemons, juiced
1 egg, lightly beaten
90 g (3^1/4 oz/^{3}/4 cup) self-raising flour
75 g (2^1/2 oz/^{1}/2 cup) polenta
^{1}/2 teaspoon baking powder
50 g (1^3/4 oz) unsalted butter
1 tablespoon olive oil
2 handfuls baby English spinach
12 slices smoked salmon
1 tablespoon salted baby capers,
   rinsed and drained

Combine the milk and half the lemon juice in a small bowl. Stir in the egg. Combine the flour, polenta, baking powder and ^{1}/2 teaspoon salt in a large bowl. Add the egg mixture and whisk until a thick batter forms, then stand for 30 minutes. Meanwhile, heat the remaining lemon juice in a saucepan over medium heat and whisk in the butter. Remove from the heat when the butter has dissolved.

Heat a non-stick frying pan over medium heat and add the olive oil. Spoon 3 tablespoons of batter into the pan for each pancake. Cook until the underside is golden brown, then flip and cook for another minute. Repeat with the remaining batter. Top each pancake with the spinach, smoked salmon, capers and lemon butter sauce.

coconut chicken salad serves 4

2 tablespoons finely chopped lemon
  grass, white part only
1 teaspoon shaved palm or soft
  brown sugar
3 tablespoons lime juice
250 ml (9 fl oz/1 cup) coconut milk
1 teaspoon sesame oil
2 skinless, boneless chicken breasts
70 g (2¹/₂ oz) mint
¹/₄ fresh coconut, flesh shaved
  and toasted
100 g (3¹/₂ oz) snow pea (mangetout)
  sprouts
2 Lebanese (short) cucumbers,
  thinly sliced
2 tablespoons sesame seeds, toasted
lime wedges, to serve

Preheat the oven to 180°C (350°F/ Gas 4). To make the dressing, combine the lemon grass, the palm sugar, 2 tablespoons of lime juice and the coconut milk in a small saucepan over low heat. Simmer for 10 minutes, stirring occasionally to ensure that the sugar has dissolved. Remove from the heat and allow to cool.

Put the sesame oil and the remaining lime juice in a small bowl. Add the chicken breasts and toss in the oil and juice before putting in a baking dish. Drizzle the chicken with the remaining marinade, cover with foil and bake in the oven for 30 minutes. Remove the chicken and allow to cool. Roughly shred the chicken and add it to the bowl with the dressing. Add the mint, coconut, sprouts and cucumber. Toss together with the sesame seeds. Serve with a wedge of lime.

smoked tofu and sesame salad

serves 4

55 g (2 oz/1/2 cup) sesame seeds,
    toasted
1 teaspoon sugar
1 1/2 tablespoons soy sauce
1 teaspoon fresh ginger juice
1 teaspoon rice vinegar
400 g (14 oz) Chinese greens or
    broccolini, cut into pieces
200 g (7 oz) smoked tofu, cut into
    cubes
2 spring onions (scallions), thinly sliced
sesame seeds, to garnish

Put the toasted sesame seeds, sugar,
soy sauce, ginger juice and vinegar in
a blender with 80 ml (2 1/2 fl oz/1/3 cup)
of water. Blend until it forms a rough
paste and put in a small bowl. Blanch
the greens in boiling salted water for
1 minute or until they turn bright green
and are tender.

Pile the cooked greens on a serving
platter with the tofu. Gently pour the
sesame dressing over the salad.
Garnish with the sliced spring onion
and a few more sesame seeds.

prawn and lemon grass soup

serves 4

12 raw king prawns (shrimp)
3 lemon grass stems
100 g (3¹/₂ oz) oyster mushrooms
100 g (3¹/₂ oz) enoki mushrooms
6 makrut (kaffir lime) leaves
2 spring onions (scallions), thinly sliced
150 g (5¹/₂ oz) bean sprouts, trimmed
3 limes, juiced
2 small red chillies
4 tablespoons fish sauce
coriander (cilantro) leaves and mint,
  to garnish

Peel and devein the prawns and set aside the shells. Cut off the white part of the lemon grass stems, reserving the tops. Cut the lemon grass stems into 2 cm (³/₄ in) lengths and flatten with a cleaver or the end of a heavy-handled knife.

Heat 1 litre (35 fl oz/4 cups) water in a saucepan. Add the prawn shells and the lemon grass tops. Bring the water to the boil, then strain into a large bowl and return the prawn stock to the saucepan. Add the crushed lemon grass, mushrooms and makrut leaves. Return to the boil, then reduce the heat to a simmer and cook for 3–4 minutes. Add the prawns and as they start to turn pink, add the spring onions, bean sprouts, lime juice, chillies and fish sauce. Stir well, then season.

Ladle into four warmed bowls. Serve with a sprinkle of coriander and mint.

steamed chicken with cashew nut and mint salad
seared prawns with mint and yoghurt chutney pancetta
and pea risotto lamb fillets with a sesame chutney
herbed chicken in paper on buttered risoni eggplant
and ricotta cheese penne slow-baked tuna with lime
leaves sesame beef winter chicken soup artichoke,
parsley and caper spaghetti ocean trout with salsa
verde teriyaki beef with wakame salad grilled chicken

03 mains

with almond salad green pea curry pan-fried whiting
thin-sliced beef with sesame roast chicken with lime
pickle zucchini and caper spaghettini chilli pork
with sugarsnap peas braised blue-eye cod spinach and
watercress stir-fry duck breast with cucumber lime

steamed chicken with cashew nut and mint salad

serves 4

3 tablespoons lime juice

1 teaspoon sugar

2 tablespoons olive oil

1 lime, peeled

1 lemon grass stem, trimmed, roughly chopped

2 garlic cloves

1 tablespoon grated fresh ginger

1 large red chilli, seeded and roughly chopped

1 1/2 tablespoons fish sauce

1/4 teaspoon ground white pepper

4 x 200 g (7 oz) skinless, boneless chicken breasts

200 g (7 oz) bean sprouts, trimmed

25 g (1 oz) Vietnamese mint, leaves picked

80 g (2 3/4 oz) roast cashews, roughly chopped

steamed rice, to serve

To make the dressing, combine the lime juice, sugar and olive oil in a bowl. Put the lime peel, lemon grass, garlic, ginger, chilli, fish sauce and white pepper in a food processor and process into a paste. Rub over the chicken before placing in a steamer basket over a pot of boiling water for 20 minutes.

Toss the sprouts and mint together and put on a serving platter. Slice the chicken across the grain and arrange over the salad. Scatter with cashews and drizzle with the dressing. Serve with steamed rice.

seared prawns with mint and yoghurt chutney serves 4

16 large raw prawns (shrimp), peeled
   and deveined with tails intact
2 tablespoons olive oil
4 tablespoons lemon juice
1 large handful mint
1 green chilli, seeded
1 teaspoon ground roast cumin
1 teaspoon sugar
1 tablespoon grated fresh ginger
5 tablespoons plain yoghurt
10 snow peas (mangetout), blanched
1 Lebanese (short) cucumber, diced
5 handfuls coriander (cilantro) leaves
steamed white rice, to serve

Toss the prawns in the olive oil and 1 tablespoon of the lemon juice.

Put the mint leaves, remaining lemon juice, green chilli, roast cumin, sugar and ginger in a blender and process to make a thin sauce. Pour the sauce into a bowl and fold through the yoghurt. Season to taste.

Heat a frying pan over high heat and sear the prawns, a few at a time, until they are beginning to change colour and curl. Turn over and cook for a further minute.

Divide the snow peas, cucumber and coriander leaves between four plates and top with the warm prawns. Drizzle with the yoghurt sauce and serve with steamed white rice.

pancetta and pea risotto

serves 4

40 g (1¹/2 oz) butter
1 onion, finely diced
8 slices pancetta, finely diced
4 sage leaves
220 g (7³/4 oz/1 cup) risotto rice
1 litre (35 fl oz/4 cups) hot chicken
    stock (basics)
150 g (5¹/2 oz/1 cup) frozen peas
75 g (2¹/2 oz/³/4 cup) grated fresh
    parmesan cheese
1 large handful flat-leaf (Italian) parsley,
    roughly chopped
10 mint leaves, finely chopped
extra virgin olive oil, for drizzling
grated fresh parmesan cheese,
    to serve

Heat the butter in a large saucepan over medium heat. Add the onion, pancetta and sage. Sauté until the onions are soft and transparent. Add the rice. Stir for 1 minute, or until it is well coated and glossy.

Add 250 ml (9 fl oz/1 cup) of stock. Simmer, stirring, until it is completely absorbed. Add more stock, and when the liquid has been absorbed, add the peas and more stock. Cook until all the liquid has been absorbed and then test the rice to see if it is *al dente*. If it needs further cooking, add a little more stock or water.

Fold in the parmesan and work it into the risotto before adding the parsley and mint at the last minute. Serve with a drizzle of extra virgin olive oil and some more parmesan.

lamb fillets with a sesame chutney

40 g (1 1/2 oz/1/4 cup) sesame seeds, toasted
1 handful coriander (cilantro) leaves
1 handful mint
3 large green chillies, seeded and finely chopped
3 tablespoons tamarind concentrate
1 tablespoon shaved palm sugar (jaggery)
1 tablespoon olive oil
8 lamb loin fillets, trimmed (about 500 g/1 lb 2 oz)
3 handfuls baby rocket (arugula)

To make the sesame chutney, put the sesame seeds, coriander, mint, chillies, tamarind, palm sugar and 4 tablespoons of water into a food processor and blend into a smooth paste. Set aside in a small bowl.

Heat the olive oil in a large frying pan over high heat. Add the lamb fillets and sear until blood begins to show on the uncooked side. Turn over and cook for a further minute. Remove from the heat and season with sea salt. Cover with foil and allow to rest for 1 minute. Slice the fillets and divide between four serving plates. Serve with a spoonful of the sesame chutney and rocket leaves.

herbed chicken in paper on buttered risoni

8 large sage leaves

1 leek, thinly sliced into 8 cm (3 in) lengths

4 skinless, boneless, chicken breasts

40 g (1½ oz) butter

400 g (14 oz) risoni

1 lemon, zest grated

3 handfuls flat-leaf (Italian) parsley, roughly chopped

Preheat the oven to 180°C (350°F/ Gas 4). Lay four 20 cm (8 in) squares of baking paper along your kitchen bench and arrange a sage leaf topped with some leek at the centre of each. Put a chicken breast on top of the leek, then season and dab with a little butter. Top with more leeks and another sage leaf and then wrap up each of the parcels. Put on a baking tray and bake for 25 minutes.

Meanwhile, cook the risoni in salted boiling water until it is *al dente*. Drain and return to the warm pan with the remaining butter, lemon zest and parsley. Stir to combine.

To serve, pile the risoni onto four warmed plates and serve the chicken either in its wrapping or turned out. Allow the chicken juices to spill over the pasta.

eggplant and ricotta cheese penne

125 ml (4 fl oz/1/2 cup) vegetable oil
1 large eggplant (aubergine), cut into
   1 cm (1/2 in) cubes
2 garlic cloves, crushed
1 onion, finely chopped
4 zucchini (courgettes), thinly sliced
100 g (31/2 oz) fresh ricotta cheese
20 basil leaves, torn
20 oregano leaves
50 g (13/4 oz) grated fresh parmesan
   cheese
400 g (14 oz) penne
2 tablespoons extra virgin olive oil

Heat a frying pan over high heat and add the vegetable oil. Fry the eggplant cubes until they are golden and soft. Remove with a slotted spoon and set aside to drain on paper towels.

Pour off most of the oil, leaving a small amount just coating the pan. Add the garlic and onion and cook over medium heat until the onion is transparent. Add the zucchini and cook until it is just beginning to soften. Put the eggplant, zucchini, ricotta, basil, oregano and parmesan in a large bowl.

Meanwhile, bring a large pot of salted water to the boil. Add the penne and cook until it is *al dente*. Drain and add to the other ingredients. Season with sea salt and freshly ground black pepper. Serve immediately with a drizzle of extra virgin olive oil.

slow-baked tuna with makrut leaves

serves 4

600 g (1 lb 5 oz) piece tuna fillet
15 makrut (kaffir lime) leaves
2 tablespoons pink peppercorns
250–500 ml (9–17 fl oz/1–2 cups) light
  olive oil
lime mayonnaise (basics), to serve
steamed potatoes and lime wedges,
  to serve

Preheat the oven to 120°C (235°F/ Gas 1/2). Trim the tuna fillet, removing any of the dark flesh, and if the fillet is particularly thick, slice it in half lengthways. Put the tuna in a loaf tin or small casserole dish. Season with some sea salt and scatter over the lime leaves and peppercorns. Pour over enough oil to cover the fillet and then seal the top with a lid or aluminium foil. Put the tuna into the oven and bake for 45 minutes.

Lift the tuna out of the oil and serve it in thick slices with steamed potatoes, lime mayonnaise and wedges of lime.

sesame beef

serves 4

500 g (1 lb 2 oz) rump steak, thinly
  sliced
1 tablespoon peanut oil
1 teaspoon sesame oil
2 garlic cloves, finely chopped
3 tablespoons hoisin sauce
3 tablespoons Chinese rice wine
1 tablespoon shaved palm or soft
  brown sugar
2 tablespoons sesame seeds
250 g (9 oz) bamboo shoots, thinly
  sliced
500 g (1 lb 2 oz) English spinach,
  washed and thinly sliced
2 large red chillies, seeded and
  chopped
1 tablespoon lemon juice
rice noodles or steamed white rice,
  to serve

Put the steak into a bowl with the peanut oil, sesame oil and garlic. Stir to coat the beef well, cover and refrigerate for a few hours or overnight. Combine the hoisin sauce, rice wine and palm sugar in a small bowl. Stir until the sugar has dissolved, then set aside. Add the beef mixture, in batches, to a hot wok and stir-fry until browned. Remove and set aside. Stir-fry the sesame seeds for 1 minute, then add the beef, bamboo shoots, spinach and chillies. Toss for 1 minute, then add the blended sauce. As the sauce begins to bubble, toss a few times, then add the lemon juice. Toss once more. Serve with fresh rice noodles or steamed rice.

winter chicken soup

2 tablespoons olive oil
2 slices bacon, finely chopped
2 onions, finely diced
1 carrot, grated
1 bay leaf
2 large potatoes, diced
3 celery stalks, thinly sliced
2 skinless, boneless chicken breasts,
    cut into small cubes
1.5 litres (52 fl oz/6 cups) chicken
    stock (basics)
1 handful flat-leaf (Italian) parsley,
    roughly chopped
90 g (3 1/4 oz/1/3 cup) sour cream
    (optional)

Put the olive oil, bacon and onions in a large saucepan. Sauté over medium heat until the bacon is nicely browned. Add the carrot, bay leaf, potatoes and celery stalks. Stir for 1 minute, then add the chicken and stock. Simmer for 30 minutes. Season according to taste with sea salt and white pepper. Add the parsley just prior to serving. For a richer version, top each serve with sour cream.

artichoke, parsley and caper spaghetti serves 4

340 g (12 oz) jar marinated artichoke
hearts, drained and finely chopped
5 handfuls flat-leaf (Italian) parsley,
roughly chopped
1 lemon, zest grated and juiced
2 tablespoons salted capers, rinsed
well
3 handfuls baby English spinach leaves
50 g (1 3/4 oz/1/2 cup) grated fresh
parmesan cheese
2 tablespoons extra virgin olive oil
400 g (14 oz) spaghetti

Bring a large pot of salted water to the boil.

Put the artichoke hearts, parsley, lemon zest, lemon juice, capers, spinach, parmesan and half the extra virgin olive oil in a bowl and stir until combined.

Cook the spaghetti in the boiling water until *al dente*, then drain and add to the bowl. Stir until the spaghetti is well coated, then drizzle with the remaining olive oil. Divide between four pasta bowls, season with freshly ground black pepper and serve immediately.

ocean trout with
salsa verde

salsa verde

**1 thick slice white bread, crusts
removed**
40 g (1½ oz) flat-leaf (Italian) parsley
4 anchovies
**1 teaspoon small capers, rinsed
and drained**
10 mint leaves
**1 tablespoon Indian lime pickle or
preserved lemon**
80 ml (2½ fl oz/⅓ cup) light olive oil

4 x 175 g (6 oz) ocean trout fillets
2 tablespoons light olive oil
boiled potatoes, to serve

To make the salsa verde, soak the bread in a bowl of water and then squeeze out any excess water — it should be soft but not wet. Put it into a food processor or blender with the parsley leaves, anchovies, capers, mint leaves, lime pickle and light olive oil and blend to form a thick sauce.

Rinse the trout fillets in cold water and pat dry with some paper towels. Heat the oil in a frying pan over high heat and add the fillets, skin side down. Press into the pan, ensuring that the heat hits the entire surface of the fillet. Cook for 2 minutes or until the skin is crisp and then turn over. Reduce the heat to medium and cook for a further 3 minutes.

Serve the seared trout with the salsa verde, boiled potatoes and a sprinkling of sea salt.

teriyaki beef with wakame salad

serves 4

450 g (1 lb) lean beef fillet, trimmed
3 tablespoons teriyaki sauce
25 g (1 oz) dried wakame seaweed
4 tablespoons rice vinegar
3 Lebanese (short) cucumbers
2 tablespoons caster (superfine) sugar
1/2 teaspoon soy sauce
3 cm (11/2 in) piece fresh ginger,
   julienned
2 red radishes, thinly sliced
1 large handful watercress sprigs
1 tablespoon black sesame seeds

Marinate the beef fillet in the teriyaki sauce for 30 minutes. Preheat the oven to 200°C (400°F/Gas 6). Heat a heavy-based frying pan over high heat and sear the fillet on all sides. Put on a baking tray and bake for 10 minutes. Remove and set aside.

Soak the wakame in cold water for 10 minutes, or until soft. Drain, put it in a bowl and cover with 1 tablespoon of the vinegar. Thinly slice the cucumbers diagonally and put in a separate bowl. Sprinkle with 1/2 teaspoon salt and set aside for several minutes. Dissolve the sugar in the soy sauce and remaining vinegar and add the ginger. Rinse the salt off the cucumber and gently squeeze dry. Combine the wakame, cucumber, radishes and dressing in a bowl. Toss to combine.

Thinly slice the beef and divide among four plates. Top with the salad and garnish with watercress and black sesame seeds.

roast chicken with almond salad

serves 4

10 saffron threads
1/2 teaspoon ground cinnamon
1 teaspoon ground ginger
2 lemons, juiced
100 ml (3 1/2 fl oz) olive oil
4 chicken leg quarters
2 green capsicums (peppers), seeded and diced
45 g (1 1/2 oz/1/2 cup) flaked almonds, toasted
1 handful flat-leaf (Italian) parsley
1 tablespoon finely chopped preserved lemon
rocket (arugula), to serve

Cover the saffron with 3 tablespoons of boiling water in a small bowl. Leave to steep for 2–3 minutes. Meanwhile, put the cinnamon, ginger, lemon juice and 4 tablespoons of the olive oil in a large bowl. Stir to combine the ingredients, then add the chicken, saffron water and freshly ground black pepper. Cover and leave to marinate in the fridge for a few hours or overnight.

Preheat the oven to 200°C (400°F/ Gas 6). Put the chicken in a baking tray, drizzle with the marinade, then season with a little sea salt. Bake for 40 minutes.

Meanwhile, heat the remaining olive oil in a frying pan over medium heat. Cook the capsicums until they begin to soften, then set aside. Add the almonds, parsley and preserved lemon to the capsicums and serve scattered over the baked chicken with rocket.

green pea curry

serves 4

2 tablespoons oil
2 teaspoons brown mustard seeds
1 teaspoon grated fresh ginger
1 large onion, thinly sliced
1 teaspoon ground cumin
1 teaspoon ground turmeric
1 red chilli, seeded and finely chopped
2 large ripe tomatoes, cut into chunks
2 tablespoons finely chopped mint
250 g (9 oz/1²/₃ cups) fresh peas
steamed white rice, to serve

Heat the oil in a deep frying pan and put in the mustard seeds. As the seeds begin to pop, add the ginger, onion and a little sea salt, and cook until the onion is soft. Mix in the cumin, turmeric and chilli, cook for 1 minute and add the tomatoes and 125 ml (4 fl oz/1/2 cup) of water. Simmer for 2 minutes. Add the mint and peas. Cover and cook for 10–15 minutes, or until the peas are tender. Add the mint. Season to taste and serve with steamed white rice.

pan-fried whiting

3 tablespoons lemon juice
125 ml (4 fl oz/1/2 cup) light olive oil
2 tablespoons finely chopped mint
2 tablespoons finely chopped dill
1 garlic clove, crushed
8 whiting fillets (about 500 g/1 lb 2 oz)
leaf salad, boiled new potatoes and
   lemon wedges, to serve

Put the lemon juice, olive oil, mint, dill and garlic in a large bowl and mix well. Rinse the whiting fillets in cold water and pat dry with paper towels. Toss the fillets in the marinade, cover and leave to marinate for a few hours in the fridge. Heat a large non-stick frying pan over high heat. Cook the whiting for 1–2 minutes on each side, then take the fillets out of the pan. Add any remaining marinade to the pan and cook for 1 minute. Serve the whiting on a leaf salad with quartered new potatoes, some of the pan juices and a lemon wedge.

thin-sliced beef
with sesame

serves 4

2 tablespoons hoisin sauce
2 tablespoons soy sauce
4 tablespoons sesame oil
40 g (1 1/2 oz/1/4 cup) sesame seeds,
  roasted
1 tablespoon honey
1 lime, juiced
1/2 teaspoon finely chopped chilli
700 g (1 lb 9 oz) roasted beef fillet
150 g (5 1/2 oz) cherry tomatoes,
  quartered
2 Lebanese (short) cucumbers, thinly
  sliced
1 small red onion, thinly sliced
3 handfuls coriander (cilantro) leaves

Combine the hoisin sauce, soy sauce, sesame oil, sesame seeds, honey, lime juice and chilli in a small bowl.

Thinly slice the beef and put it in a large bowl. Add half of the sauce and the remaining salad ingredients and toss them together. Arrange the salad in piles on four bowls and drizzle with the remaining sauce.

roast chicken with lime pickle

serves 4

1.8 kg (4 lb) free-range chicken
1 lemon, halved
1 onion, quartered
40 g (1 1/2 oz) butter
3 tablespoons Indian lime pickle,
   finely chopped
1 handful watercress sprigs
mashed potato and lime wedges,
   to serve

Preheat the oven to 200°C (400°F/ Gas 6). Rinse the chicken and pat it dry with paper towels. Put the chicken in a roasting tin, breast side up, and stuff with the lemon and onion. Push the butter under the skin of the chicken breast. Rub the lime pickle over the chicken and lightly season with sea salt. Bake for 1 1/4 hours, or until cooked through. Remove the chicken and check that it is cooked by pulling a leg away from the body — the juices that run out should be clear and not pink. Allow to rest for 15 minutes before carving and serving on a plates. Drizzle with some of the pan juices and garnish with watercress sprigs. Serve with mashed potato and lime wedges.

zucchini and caper spaghettini

serves 4

3 tablespoons extra virgin olive oil
2 garlic cloves, crushed
6 zucchini (courgettes), grated
400 g (14 oz) spaghettini
1 large handful flat-leaf (Italian) parsley,
    roughly chopped
2 tablespoons small capers, rinsed
    and drained
110 g (3³/4 oz/1 heaped cup) grated
    fresh parmesan cheese

Bring a large saucepan of salted water to the boil for the pasta. Heat a deep frying pan over medium heat. Add the olive oil and garlic. Move the garlic around the pan with a spatula until it is lightly golden, then add the zucchini. Slowly braise the zucchini, stirring it as it cooks, for about 15 minutes, or until it begins to dry out and catch on the bottom of the pan.

Cook the pasta until it is *al dente*, then drain and return to the saucepan. Add the parsley, capers, most of the parmesan and the zucchini. Toss together and divide the pasta between four pasta bowls. Sprinkle with the remaining parmesan.

steamed barramundi with warm greens

serves 4

1 tablespoon ground roast cumin
1 teaspoon thyme
1/2 teaspoon ground turmeric
1 teaspoon sea salt
4 x 200 g (7 oz) barramundi fillets
60 g (21/4 oz) butter
3 zucchini (courgettes), sliced on
   the diagonal
150 g (51/2 oz) sugar snap peas,
   trimmed
1 tablespoon lemon juice

Put a large saucepan of water on to boil for the steamer. Tip the cumin, thyme, turmeric, sea salt and some ground black pepper into a clean plastic bag. Rinse the barramundi fillets in cold water and pat dry with paper towels. Add the fish fillets to the bag and shake the bag to coat the fish in the spices.

Melt the butter in a large frying pan over medium heat. Add the zucchini and sauté until they are beginning to soften. Add the sugar snaps and lemon juice. Cover the pan for a few minutes, allowing the peas to steam to a bright green.

Put the fish on a plate in a steamer basket. Cook over simmering water for 4–5 minutes. Serve the fish with the lemony greens.

chilli pork with sugar snap peas

serves 4

3 tablespoons hoisin sauce
2 tablespoons Chinese rice wine
1 tablespoon finely grated fresh ginger
1/2 teaspoon red chilli flakes
2 teaspoons sesame oil
1 garlic clove, crushed
400 g (14 oz) pork fillet, thinly sliced
1 tablespoon peanut oil
1 red capsicum (pepper), thinly sliced
300 g (10 1/2 oz) sugar snap peas,
   trimmed
90 g (3 1/4 oz) bean sprouts, trimmed
basil, to garnish
steamed rice or warm noodles,
   to serve

Combine the hoisin sauce, rice wine, ginger, red chilli flakes, sesame oil and garlic in a large bowl. Stir to blend, then add the sliced pork. Stir several times to coat the pork. Cover and refrigerate for several hours. Remove the pork and reserve the marinade.

Heat the peanut oil in a hot wok. Stir-fry the capsicum and sugar snap peas until the capsicum is beginning to soften. Remove from the pan and set aside. Stir-fry the pork, in batches, until brown. Return all of the pork and vegetables to the wok along with the bean sprouts and the reserved marinade. Continue to stir-fry until the sauce begins to bubble. Garnish with basil leaves and serve with steamed rice or warm noodles.

braised blue-eye cod serves 4

4 x 200 g (7 oz) blue-eye cod fillets
   or cod fillets
1 tablespoon olive oil
2 garlic cloves, thinly sliced
4 spring onions (scallions), thinly sliced
2 tablespoons finely chopped dill
250 ml (9 fl oz/1 cup) white wine
1 lemon, zested and juiced
1 large handful roughly chopped
   flat-leaf (Italian) parsley
20 g (3/4 oz) butter
steamed snow peas (mangetout),
   to serve

Rinse the fish fillets in cold water and pat dry with paper towels. Rub the fillets with salt and white pepper.

Heat the oil in a non-stick frying pan and sauté the garlic until it is lightly golden. Add the spring onions, dill, white wine, lemon zest and lemon juice and bring to the boil.

Add the fish and cover the pan. Reduce the heat and simmer for 8 minutes. Remove the fish pieces from the cooking liquid and arrange on a warmed serving platter. Return the pan to high heat and boil until the liquid has reduced by half. Add the parsley and butter, swirling the frying pan until the butter has melted. Pour the sauce over the fish. Serve with steamed snow peas.

spinach and watercress stir-fry

1 tablespoon vegetable oil

2 tablespoons finely chopped lemon grass, white part only

1 small red chilli, seeded and thinly chopped

2 red capsicums (peppers), thinly sliced

90 g (3^1/$_4$ oz/^{1}/$_2$ cup) tinned water chestnuts, roughly chopped

500 g (1 lb 2 oz) English spinach, thinly sliced

400 g (14 oz) watercress, stems removed

1 tablespoon light soy sauce

1 teaspoon soft brown sugar

1 tablespoon fish sauce

steamed jasmine rice or white noodles, to serve

Heat the oil in a wok or large frying pan over medium to high heat. Add the lemon grass and chilli and cook for 1 minute before adding the capsicums. Cook the capsicums for a further minute before adding the water chestnuts, spinach and watercress.

Stir-fry for 1 minute, or until the leaves are beginning to wilt. Add the soy sauce, sugar and fish sauce. Toss together. Serve with steamed jasmine rice or slippery white noodles.

duck breast with cucumber

115 g (4 oz/1/2 cup) soft brown sugar
3 teaspoons grated fresh ginger
1 orange, zest grated, juiced
4 boneless duck breasts
2 teaspoons sesame oil
3 teaspoons sesame seeds
6 Lebanese (short) cucumbers, halved
  and sliced on the diagonal
80 g (2¾ oz) garlic chives, cut
  into lengths
1 tablespoon soy sauce
rice, to serve

Put the brown sugar, 2 teaspoons of grated ginger and the orange zest in a bowl and mix together. With a sharp knife, make several diagonal cuts across the skin of the duck breast. Rub the sugar mixture into the surface of the skin. Marinate for several hours or overnight in the fridge.

Preheat the oven to 180°C (350°F/ Gas 4). Put the duck breasts in a roasting tin. Roast for 10–12 minutes. Remove the duck, cover and keep warm. Heat the sesame oil in a wok and add the sesame seeds and remaining ginger. As soon as the seeds begin to brown, add the cucumber and chives. Toss for 1 minute, then add the soy, orange juice and duck juices.

Put the duck under a hot grill (broiler) for a minute to crisp up the skin. Serve the breasts sliced over the cucumber with rice.

lime-marinated fish   serves 4

2 makrut (kaffir lime) leaves, thinly
   sliced
2 limes, juiced
1 red chilli, seeded and finely chopped
1 teaspoon fish sauce
2 tablespoons grated fresh ginger
3 tablespoons olive oil
80 g (2³/4 oz) coriander (cilantro)
4 x 150 g (5¹/2 oz) blue-eye cod fillets
tomato rice (basics)

Put the makrut leaves, lime juice, chilli, fish sauce, ginger and olive oil in a large bowl. Stir to combine. Remove the stems and roots from the coriander and wash carefully. Finely chop and stir into the marinade. Add the fish and toss until well coated. Cover and leave in the fridge to marinate.

Heat a frying pan over medium heat and add the fish fillets. Sear on one side for 3 minutes before turning the fillets over and cooking for a further 3 minutes, or until they are cooked through.

Put a large spoonful of the tomato rice on each of the serving plates. Garnish with the coriander leaves and top with the fish fillets.

poached chicken with coriander

40 g (1 1/2 oz) coriander (cilantro)
3 lemons
1 tablespoon sea salt
4 skinless, boneless chicken breasts
75 g (2 1/2 oz) flat-leaf (Italian) parsley
1 garlic clove
125 ml (4 fl oz/1/2 cup) olive oil
2 Lebanese (short) cucumbers, cut
   into chunks
leaf salad, to serve

Remove the roots and stems from the coriander and put them into a large pot of water. Add the juice of one lemon and the sea salt and bring to the boil. When the water is boiling, put in the chicken. Cover the pot with a tight-fitting lid and remove it from the heat. Leave covered for 1 hour.

To make the dressing put half the coriander leaves, the parsley, garlic and the juice of the two remaining lemons into a blender or food processor. Blend everything together while slowly pouring in the olive oil. Season to taste.

When the chicken is cooked, drain and slice thinly across the grain. Toss the chicken with the dressing, cucumbers and coriander leaves. Serve with a leaf salad.

salmon fillets with a tamarind sauce

serves 4

3 tablespoons tamarind water (basics)
1 teaspoon fish sauce
1 teaspoon sesame oil
1 teaspoon soy sauce
1 teaspoon honey
4 x 140 g (5 oz) salmon fillets, skin removed
1 tablespoon sesame seeds
steamed rice, coriander (cilantro) leaves and lime wedges, to serve

Put the tamarind water, fish sauce, sesame oil, soy sauce and honey in a large glass or plastic bowl and stir together. Rinse the salmon fillets in cold water and pat dry with paper towels. Add to the tamarind mixture. Cover and marinate for 1 hour or overnight in the fridge.

Heat a non-stick frying pan over a high heat and sear the fillets, shaking off any excess marinade before you put them in the pan. When the fillets begin to brown, flip over and reduce the heat.

Pour the remaining marinade into the pan and sprinkle the tops of the fillets with sesame seeds. Simmer the fillets for 5–8 minutes, or until they are just cooked through and the marinade has reduced to a thick sauce. Serve with rice, coriander leaves and lime wedges.

barley risotto with
wilted greens

serves 4

40 g (1¹/2 oz) butter
2 garlic cloves, crushed
1 tablespoon thyme
3 onions, thinly sliced
220 g (7³/4 oz/1 cup) pearl barley
1 lemon, zest grated
1 litre (35 fl oz/4 cups) chicken stock
  (basics)
70 g (2¹/2 oz/²/3 cup) grated fresh
  parmesan cheese
1 tablespoon olive oil
900 g (2 lb) kale or water spinach,
  roughly chopped
grated fresh parmesan cheese,
  to serve

Heat the butter in a large saucepan over medium heat and add the garlic and thyme. When the garlic begins to soften, add the onions and cook until they are soft. Mix in the pearl barley and lemon zest. Stir for a few minutes until the barley is well coated and glistening.

Add 250 ml (9 fl oz/1 cup) of stock and simmer, stirring until the stock has been absorbed. Continue to add the stock a little at a time until it has all been taken up by the pearl barley. Just as the last of the stock has been absorbed, stir in the grated parmesan. Meanwhile, heat a frying pan or wok over high heat and add the olive oil. Toss in the kale and quickly stir-fry until the greens are just cooked. Spoon the risotto into four warmed bowls, then top with some of the greens. Serve with extra parmesan.

stir-fried king prawns

serves 4

3 tablespoons peanut oil

800 g (1 lb 12 oz) raw king prawns (shrimp), peeled and deveined with tails intact

3 cm (1¼ in) piece fresh ginger, peeled and julienned

2 red capsicums (peppers), thinly sliced

2 yellow capsicums (peppers), thinly sliced

2 zucchini (courgettes), thinly sliced lengthways and sliced diagonally into thin strips

4 tablespoons Chinese rice wine

2 tablespoons soy sauce

1 teaspoon sesame oil

lime wedges and garlic chives, to garnish

steamed rice, to serve

Heat the peanut oil in a hot wok and stir-fry the prawns for 1 minute. Add the ginger, capsicums and zucchini and stir-fry for a further 1 minute. Add the rice wine and simmer for 1 minute. Add the soy sauce and sesame oil. Toss for a further 1 minute and then remove from the heat. Garnish with lime wedges and garlic chives and serve with steamed rice.

mint and makrut chicken

4 x 200 g (7 oz) skinless, boneless
    chicken breasts
8 makrut (kaffir lime) leaves
2 tablespoons shaved palm sugar
    (jaggery)
1 garlic clove
2 teaspoons fish sauce
15 mint leaves
3 tablespoons olive oil
coriander (cilantro), to garnish
250 g (9 oz) sugar snap peas, trimmed,
    blanched and sliced on the diagonal
steamed rice, to serve

Slice the chicken breasts into four pieces lengthways and put in a bowl. Using a pair of kitchen scissors, finely cut the makrut leaves and put them in a food processor or blender with the palm sugar, garlic, fish sauce, mint leaves and olive oil. Process for 1 minute. Pour the marinade over the chicken and stir so the chicken is well coated. Cover and put in the fridge to marinate for 1 hour, or overnight. Heat a non-stick frying pan or barbecue and cook the chicken pieces for a few minutes each side. Garnish with coriander and serve with the sugar snap peas and steamed rice.

steak with caramelized
rosemary shallots   serves 4

20 g (³/₄ oz) butter
200 g (7 oz) baby onions or French
   shallots, sliced in half if large
4 sprigs rosemary
1 teaspoon sugar
185 ml (6 fl oz/³/₄ cup) red wine
1 teaspoon balsamic vinegar
1 teaspoon olive oil
4 x 200 g (7 oz) fillet steaks
mashed potato, to serve

Heat the butter in a saucepan over medium heat and add the onions. Toss the onions around until they are golden and beginning to soften. Add the rosemary and cook until the shallots are caramelized on the outside. Add the sugar and swirl it around the pan until it has dissolved. Pour in the red wine and balsamic vinegar. Allow the sauce to simmer for a couple of minutes to reduce the liquid by half.

Heat a heavy cast-iron frying pan over high heat and add the olive oil. As it begins to smoke, add the steaks and sear them until the uncooked surface begins to look slightly bloody. Turn each of the steaks over and cook for a further minute. Season and allow the steak to rest for a few minutes in the pan. Spoon the onions over and serve with a dollop of mashed potato.

whiting fillets with herb butter

1 handful flat-leaf (Italian) parsley
2 tablespoons chopped chives
1 garlic clove, chopped
2 gherkins (pickles), chopped
3 anchovies
1 tablespoon salted capers, rinsed
and drained
1/4 teaspoon white pepper
100 g (3 1/2 oz) butter, softened
1 teaspoon olive oil
8 whiting fillets (about 500 g/1 lb 2 oz)
400 g (14 oz) watercress, sprigs picked

Put the parsley, chives, garlic, gherkins, anchovies, capers, white pepper and butter into a food processor or blender and process until a smooth paste forms. Lay a large piece of plastic wrap on a clean surface and spoon the flavoured butter in a line. Roll up to form a log and refrigerate until you are ready to use it.

Heat the olive oil in a large non-stick frying pan over high heat. Cook the whiting for 1–2 minutes on each side, then remove from the pan. Serve on a bed of watercress topped with a few slices of the herbed butter.

winter vegetable chicken

serves 2

30 g (1 oz/1/4 cup) plain (all-purpose)
  flour
2 teaspoons sea salt
1 teaspoon ground roast cumin
2 chicken drumsticks
2 chicken thighs
1 carrot, peeled and cut into small
  chunks
1 turnip, peeled and cut into small
  chunks
1 parsnip, peeled and cut into small
  chunks
1 onion, sliced
2 celery stalks, trimmed and sliced
1 leek, washed and sliced
250 ml (9 fl oz/1 cup) chicken stock
  (basics) or water
roughly chopped flat-leaf (Italian)
  parsley, to serve

Preheat the oven to 180°C (350°F/ Gas 4). Put the flour and seasonings into a bowl and toss the chicken pieces so that they are well covered with the seasoned flour.

Put half the vegetables into the base of a casserole dish and then top with the chicken (shake off any excess seasoning). Add the remaining vegetables and stock, cover the dish with a lid or foil and put in the oven for 1 hour 20 minutes. Remove and serve immediately with a scattering of freshly chopped parsley.

steamed fish with cucumber and herbs

serves 4

2 lemon grass stems, finely chopped

60 g (2¹/₄ oz/¹/₄ cup) caster (superfine) sugar

4 tablespoons fish sauce

4 x 200 g (7 oz) white fish fillets, sliced into thick strips

1 red chilli, seeded and finely chopped

2 teaspoons finely grated fresh ginger

4 tablespoons lime juice

1 tablespoon fish sauce

1 tablespoon shaved palm sugar (jaggery)

1 large handful mint

1 large handful coriander (cilantro) leaves

1¹/₂ handfuls basil

3 Lebanese (short) cucumbers, cut into chunks

Put the lemon grass in a bowl with the sugar and fish sauce and add the fish pieces. Toss the fish in the sauce mixture to coat each piece well, and leave to marinate.

Put the chilli, ginger, lime juice, fish sauce and sugar in a bowl. Stir until the sugar has dissolved. Add the fresh herbs and cucumber and put the salad on a serving platter. Put the fish pieces on a plate in a bamboo or metal steamer basket and put the basket over a saucepan of simmering water. Cover and steam for 3–4 minutes. Toss the fish gently through the salad while it is hot.

lemon and thyme lamb cutlets

20 g (3/4 oz) lemon thyme
12 lamb cutlets, French trimmed
3 tablespoons lemon juice
3 tablespoons olive oil
560 g (1 lb 4 oz) kipfler (fingerling)
   or salad potatoes
80 g (23/4 oz/3/4 cup) black olives
1 large handful flat-leaf (Italian) parsley,
   chopped
3 tablespoons olive oil
green salad, to serve

Put half of the lemon thyme into a container and lay the lamb cutlets on top. Cover with the remaining thyme, the lemon juice and the olive oil, making sure the cutlets are well coated in the marinade. Leave to marinate for at least 1 hour or preferably overnight in the fridge.

Cut the potatoes into big chunks. Put them in a large saucepan of salted cold water and bring to the boil over high heat. When the water has reached boiling point, cover the pan with a lid and remove it from the heat. Leave the potatoes to sit for half an hour. Take the cutlets out of the marinade and barbecue or grill for 2–3 minutes on each side, then allow to rest. Drain the potatoes and return to the pan along with the olives, parsley and olive oil, stirring vigorously so that the potatoes are well coated and begin to break up a little. Season to taste. Serve the cutlets with the smashed potatoes and a green salad.

swordfish with green beans

serves 4

3 tablespoons lemon juice
125 ml (4 fl oz/1/2 cup) extra virgin olive oil
1 garlic clove, crushed
1 tablespoon lemon thyme
300 g (101/2 oz) green beans, trimmed
4 x 200 g (7 oz) swordfish steaks
2 tablespoons light olive oil

Mix the lemon juice, extra virgin olive oil, garlic and lemon thyme together in a small bowl.

Bring a large saucepan of salted water to the boil. Add the green beans and cook them for 1–2 minutes, until they are emerald green and just cooked through. Drain and refresh under cold running water. Season the swordfish steaks liberally with sea salt.

Put the light olive oil in a large frying pan over high heat. Add the swordfish steaks to the pan and sear for 3 minutes, or until golden brown. Turn over, reduce the heat and leave for a further 3–4 minutes, or until they are cooked through.

Put a swordfish steak on each plate and drizzle with the lemon thyme dressing. Top the fish with some green beans and season with freshly ground black pepper.

ceviche salad

500 g (1 lb 2 oz) white fish fillets
125 ml (4 fl oz/1/2 cup) lime juice
3 tablespoons coconut cream
1 teaspoon sugar
1 red capsicum (pepper), thinly sliced
4 spring onions (scallions), thinly sliced
on the diagonal
1 large red chilli, seeded and finely
chopped
2 tomatoes, seeded and diced
2 avocados, diced
80 g (23/4 oz) coriander (cilantro)
leaves, roughly chopped

Slice the fish fillets into thin strips and put them in a glass bowl with the lime juice. Turn them over so that they are completely coated in the juice. Cover the fish and leave it to marinate and 'cook' in the fridge for 2 hours.

Drain the fish and toss it with the remaining ingredients. Divide the salad between four plates.

roast chicken with almond sauce

serves 4

4 whole chicken leg quarters
2 tablespoons olive oil
8 sprigs lemon thyme
leaf salad, to serve

almond sauce
625 ml (21¹/2 fl oz/2¹/2 cups) chicken
    stock (basics)
100 g (3¹/2 oz/1 cup) ground almonds
1 garlic clove, crushed
2 tablespoons finely chopped flat-leaf
    (Italian) parsley
¹/2 teaspoon sugar
1 lemon, juiced
1 pinch saffron

Preheat the oven to 200°C (400°F/ Gas 6). Rub sea salt into the skin of the chicken legs before putting in a roasting tin. Drizzle the chicken legs with olive oil. Cover with the thyme. Roast for 40 minutes, or until the chicken is cooked through. Remove the chicken from the oven and allow to rest for a minute.

Meanwhile, bring the stock and ground almonds to the boil in a saucepan. Reduce to a simmer, season to taste with sea salt and white pepper and add the remaining ingredients. Simmer gently for a further 20 minutes before spooning the sauce over the roast chicken. Serve with a leaf salad.

seared salmon with green mango salad

serves 4

2 tablespoons tamarind purée
2 tablespoons finely grated fresh
  ginger
1 tablespoon olive oil
4 x 100 g (3¹/₂ oz) salmon fillets
3 tablespoons lime juice
3 tablespoons fish sauce
3 tablespoons sugar
2 green mangoes
4 handfuls snow pea (mangetout)
  shoots

Put the tamarind purée, ginger and olive oil in a small bowl and stir to combine. Toss the salmon in the mixture and allow to marinate for 30 minutes.

To make the green mango salad, combine the lime juice, fish sauce and sugar in a bowl and stir until the sugar has dissolved. Peel the mangoes and finely julienne or grate the flesh. Add to the bowl with the dressing.

Heat a non-stick pan over medium heat and cook the salmon pieces for 2 minutes each side. Serve with the salad and snow pea shoots.

coconut prawns with mint and lemon grass

serves 4

2 tablespoons finely chopped
lemon grass, white part only
2 tablespoons lime juice
1/2 teaspoon shaved palm sugar
(jaggery)
250 ml (9 fl oz/1 cup) coconut milk
1 tablespoon peanut oil
20 raw king prawns (shrimp), peeled
and deveined with tails intact
80 g (2³/4 oz) mint
60 g (2¹/4 oz/1 cup) shredded coconut,
toasted
100 g (3¹/2 oz) bean sprouts, trimmed
2 Lebanese (short) cucumbers, thinly
sliced
1 lime wedges, to serve

Put the lemon grass, lime juice, sugar and coconut milk into a small saucepan over low heat. Simmer for 10 minutes, stirring occasionally to ensure the sugar dissolves. Remove from the heat and allow to cool in a large bowl.

Put a heavy-based frying pan over high heat and add the oil. Swirl the oil over the base of the pan, then add a few of the prawns. Cook only as many prawns as will comfortably fit into the pan. Sear the prawns for a few minutes on each side, flipping them over as they change colour. As the prawns are cooked, remove and add to the coconut sauce in the bowl. Continue until all the prawns are cooked. Put the mint, toasted coconut, bean sprouts and cucumber in a bowl and toss together. Pile the salad mixture onto four plates and top with the prawns. Drizzle with whatever sauce remains in the bowl and serve with lime wedges.

lemon grass chicken   serves 4

1 lime, zest grated, juiced
1 lemon grass stem, trimmed and
  roughly chopped
2 garlic cloves, peeled
2 cm (3/4 in) piece fresh ginger, peeled
  and roughly chopped
1 large red chilli, seeded
1 1/2 tablespoons fish sauce
4 skinless, boneless chicken breasts
2 tablespoons olive oil
steamed white rice and Chinese
  greens, to serve

Preheat the oven to 200°C (400°F/ Gas 6). Put the lime zest, lemon grass, garlic, ginger, chilli and fish sauce in a food processor or mortar and pestle and process or grind to a smooth paste. Rub the paste all over the chicken breasts and put in a roasting tin. Drizzle with the olive oil and lime juice. Season with a little sea salt. Cover with aluminium foil and bake for 25–30 minutes. Remove from the oven and use the pointed end of a sharp knife to check that the chicken is cooked through.

Serve sliced with steamed white rice, Chinese greens and a drizzle of baking juices. You can also toss the sliced chicken with a leaf salad and sprinkle with some ground roasted peanuts.

mushroom and tofu stir-fry

serves 4

4 dried shiitake mushrooms

4 tablespoons vegetable oil

200 g (7 oz) firm tofu, cut into 2 cm (3/4 in) cubes

1 teaspoon sesame oil

2 garlic cloves, finely chopped

3 spring onions (scallions), finely sliced

1 large red chilli, seeded and finely chopped

125 g (4 1/2 oz) snow peas (mangetout), trimmed

100 g (3 1/2 oz) oyster mushrooms, chopped

500 g (1 lb 2 oz) watercress, sprigs removed

1 tablespoon light soy sauce

2 tablespoons hoisin sauce

1 tablespoon fish sauce

Soak the dried shiitake mushrooms in 125 ml (4 fl oz/1/2 cup) hot water. Drain the shiitake mushrooms, reserving the soaking water, then remove the tough stalks and thinly slice the mushrooms. Heat 3 tablespoons of the vegetable oil in a wok. Fry the tofu over medium to high heat until golden. Remove and drain on paper towels. Wipe the wok clean. Heat the remaining vegetable oil and the sesame oil over medium heat. Add the garlic, spring onions and chilli. Stir-fry for 1 minute. Add the remaining vegetables a handful at a time, stirring constantly.

Add the light soy sauce, hoisin sauce, fish sauce and the reserved mushroom soaking water to the wok. Stir to combine. Cover and simmer for 3 minutes. Stir in the fried tofu, and gently toss the stir-fry. Serve with steamed rice or fried noodles.

bircher muesli lime madeleines drunken grapes apple
and pecan crumble cake baked apples lemon and mint
granita with shaved melon lime syrup puddings pear
and ginger cake pear and cardamom tart apple tart
bircher muesli lime madeleines drunken grapes apple
and pecan crumble cake baked apples lemon and mint
granita with shaved melon lime syrup puddings pear
and ginger cake pear and cardamom tart apple tart

04   sweets

bircher muesli lime madeleines drunken grapes apple
and pecan crumble cake baked apples lemon and mint
granita with shaved melon lime syrup puddings pear
and ginger cake pear and cardamom tart apple tart
bircher muesli lime madeleines drunken grapes apple

bircher muesli

serves 4

200 g (7 oz/2 cups) rolled (porridge)
  oats
250 ml (9 fl oz/1 cup) apple juice
2 green apples, grated
125 g (4 1/2 oz/1/2 cup) plain yoghurt
1/2 teaspoon ground cinnamon
fresh berries or stewed rhubarb,
  to serve

Put the rolled oats and apple juice in a bowl and soak for at least 1 hour or overnight. Add the grated apple to the soaked oats with the yoghurt and cinnamon. Mix well and serve with fresh berries or stewed rhubarb.

lime madeleines

makes 36

2 eggs

55 g (2 oz/¼ cup) caster (superfine) sugar, plus extra, to serve

½ teaspoon finely chopped lime zest

60 g (2¼ oz/½ cup) plain (all-purpose) flour

50 g (1¾ oz) unsalted butter, melted

1 teaspoon lime juice

½ teaspoon orange flower water

Preheat the oven to 200°C (400°F/ Gas 6). Beat the eggs, caster sugar, lime zest and a pinch of salt in a bowl until the mixture is pale and thick. Sift the flour over the egg mixture and lightly fold it in. Gently fold through the butter, lime juice and orange flower water.

Grease a madeleine tin and drop a teaspoon of the batter into each of the moulds. If you don't have a madeleine tin, use a shallow muffin or patty cake tin. Bake for 5 minutes. Repeat with any remaining mixture. Turn out onto a wire rack and sprinkle with caster sugar.

drunken grapes

500 g (1 lb 2 oz) green seedless grapes
3 tablespoons soft brown sugar
4 tablespoons vodka
4 tablespoons crème fraîche
45 g (1 1/2 oz/1/2 cup) almond flakes, toasted

Slice the grapes in half and put in a non-metallic bowl. Add the brown sugar, vodka and crème fraîche and stir. Cover the grapes with plastic wrap. Refrigerate for several hours.

Spoon the chilled grapes into four dessert bowls and top with the toasted almonds.

apple and pecan
crumble cake

250 g (9 oz/2 cups) plain (all-purpose)
  flour
2 teaspoons baking powder
370 g (13 oz/2 cups) soft brown sugar
2 teaspoons ground cinnamon
125 g (4½ oz) unsalted butter
125 ml (4 fl oz/½ cup) milk
2 eggs
100 g (3½ oz/1 cup) pecan nuts,
  chopped
2 green apples, peeled and thinly sliced
whipped cream or yoghurt, to serve

Preheat the oven to 180°C (350°F/ Gas 4). Line a 20 cm (8 in) springform tin with baking paper. Combine the flour, baking powder, sugar and cinnamon in a food processor, then add the butter and whiz until the mixture begins to resemble breadcrumbs. Put half of this mixture into the lined tin.

Add the milk and the eggs to the processor with the remaining mixture and blend again to make a batter, then fold in the chopped pecans. Scatter the sliced apple over the crumble base and cover with the batter. Bake for 1 hour and test with a skewer to see if the cake is cooked through.

Allow the cake to cool before turning it out onto a serving plate. Serve slightly warm with whipped cream or yoghurt.

baked apples with panettone

2 small panettone (about 100 g/3½ oz
    each) or 1 large one
2 tablespoons unsalted butter
4 large green apples
40 g (1½ oz) brown sugar
icing (confectioners') sugar, to serve
thick cream or vanilla custard, to serve

Preheat the oven to 180°C (350°F/ Gas 4). Line a baking tray with baking paper. Trim off the rounded top of one of the small panettone. Slice the cake into four rounds, or cut four rounds from four slices of a large panettone. Place the rounds on the baking tray and lightly butter.

Core the apples with an apple corer or a small sharp knife, making sure that you remove all the tough core pieces. Slice and butter the other small panettone, or some of the large one, before tearing it into small pieces. Stuff the small buttered panettone pieces into the centre of the apples, alternating the pieces with a little brown sugar.

Top with a teaspoon of brown sugar per apple and a dob of butter. Put the apples onto the four panettone rounds and bake for 40 minutes.

Serve warm, dusted with icing sugar and accompanied with thick cream or vanilla custard.

lemon and mint granita with shaved melon

serves 6

230 g (8¹/₂ oz/1 cup) caster (superfine) sugar
250 ml (9 oz/1 cup) lemon juice
1 teaspoon orange flower water
10 mint leaves, finely chopped
1/4 each of 1 champagne melon and 1 seedless watermelon

Put the sugar in a saucepan with 500 ml (17 fl oz/2 cups) of water and heat until the sugar has dissolved. Stir in the lemon juice, orange flower water and mint leaves and pour the mixture into a large plastic container. Freeze the granita for 3 hours, then break it up with a fork and re-freeze it.

Slice the melons into very thin slices. Alternating the two kinds of melon, make a small stack of slices on each of the six plates. Take the granita out of the freezer, break it up with a fork again and spoon it over the melon.

lime syrup puddings   serves 6

4 tablespoons golden or maple syrup
3 tablespoons lime juice
1 lime, zested
2 eggs, separated
125 g (4½ oz) unsalted butter
115 g (4 oz/½ cup) dark brown sugar
1 teaspoon natural vanilla extract
155 g (5½ oz/1¼ cups) plain
   (all-purpose) flour
1½ teaspoons ground ginger
1 teaspoon cream of tartar
½ teaspoon bicarbonate of soda
   (baking soda)
125 ml (4 fl oz/½ cup) milk
cream (whipping), to serve

Preheat the oven to 180°C (350°F/ Gas 4). Grease six 150 ml (5 fl oz) ramekins. Mix the golden syrup, lime juice and zest together in a small bowl. Divide the mixture between the moulds. Beat the egg whites until stiff and then set aside. Cream the butter and sugar together, then add the egg yolks and vanilla. Fold in the flour, ginger, cream of tartar and bicarbonate of soda alternately with the milk. Lightly fold through the beaten egg whites. Spoon the batter into the ramekins and cover with circles of baking paper. Put the ramekins into a baking tray and fill with water until it reaches halfway up the sides of the ramekins. Bake for 40 minutes, or until the puddings are cooked through. Upturn the puddings onto six plates and drizzle with cream.

pear and ginger cake   serves 8

40 g (1¹/2 oz) unsalted butter
55 g (2 oz/¹/2 cup) ground almonds
3 eggs
125 ml (4 fl oz/¹/2 cup) milk
400 g (14 oz/1³/4 cups) caster
    (superfine) sugar
1 tablespoon grated fresh ginger
250 g (9 oz/2 cups) plain (all-purpose)
    flour
2 teaspoons baking powder
3–5 beurre bosc pears, cored and
    sliced lengthways
icing (confectioners') sugar, for dusting
cream (whipping), to serve

Preheat the oven to 180°C (350°F/ Gas 4). Butter a round 20 cm (8 in) springform cake tin with half the butter. Sprinkle in half of the ground almonds and shake them around so that they stick to the buttered cake tin. Put the eggs, milk, sugar, ginger, flour and baking powder into a food processor or large bowl and process or mix to make a thick batter. Fold the pears into the batter and then spoon the mixture into the cake tin. Sprinkle the top of the batter with the remaining ground almonds and dot with the rest of the butter.

Bake for 1¹/2 hours, check to see if it is cooked through, then remove and cool. Dust with icing sugar and serve with cream.

pear and cardamom tart serves 8

185 g (6¹/₂ oz/1³/₄ cups) ground
    almonds
110 g (3³/₄ oz) unsalted butter
125 g (4¹/₂ oz) caster (superfine) sugar
3 eggs
¹/₂ teaspoon ground cardamom
3 teaspoons unsweetened cocoa
    powder
1 x 25 cm (10 in) pre-baked shortcrust
    pastry case (basics)
2 ripe beurre bosc pears

Preheat the oven to 180°C (350°F/ Gas 4). Put the ground almonds, butter, all the sugar except for 2 tablespoons, the eggs, cardamom and cocoa in a food processor and blend to form a thick paste. Carefully spoon and spread the mixture into the pre-baked pastry case.

Quarter and core the pears, then slice thickly, arranging the slices in a fan over the top of the almond mixture. Bake for 20 minutes.

Take the tart out of the oven and sprinkle the top with the rest of the sugar. Return it to the oven for a further 10 minutes and then test to check that the tart is cooked all the way through. Allow it to cool slightly before transferring it to a serving plate.

apple tartlets

makes 6

100 g (3¹/₂ oz) unsalted butter
115 g (4 oz/¹/₂ cup) sugar
1 teaspoon ground cinnamon
2 green apples, grated
1 teaspoon lemon juice
2 eggs
4 pre-baked 10 cm (4 in) tart case
   (basics)

Preheat the oven to 180°C (350°F/ Gas 4). Melt together the butter and sugar. Put into a bowl with the cinnamon, apple, lemon juice and eggs and fold together. Pour into the pre-baked tart cases and bake for 30 minutes, or until golden brown.

honeydew and pineapple whip iced lychee and mint
classic daiquiri mint and ice cream smoothie mojito
tropical rum blend margarita martini mint julep opal
ice moroccan mint tea lychee and rum blast honeydew
and pineapple whip iced lychee and mint classic
daiquiri mint and ice cream smoothie mojito tropical
rum blend margarita martini mint julep opal ice
moroccan mint tea lychee and rum blast honeydew and

05   drinks

pineapple whip iced lychee and mint   classic
daiquiri mint and ice cream smoothie mojito
tropical rum blend margarita martini mint julep
opal ice moroccan mint tea lychee and rum blast
honeydew and pineapple whip iced lychee and mint

honeydew and pineapple whip

serves 2

250 ml (9 fl oz/1 cup) fresh pineapple
  juice
175 g (2¹/2 oz/1 cup) chopped
  honeydew melon
1 tablespoon lime juice
6 ice cubes

Put the pineapple juice, honeydew melon, lime juice and ice cubes in a blender. Blend until smooth and pour into glasses.

iced lychee and mint

5 tinned lychees, drained, reserving 125 ml (4 fl oz/¹/₂ cup) of the syrup
15 large mint leaves
1 tablespoon lime juice
10 ice cubes

Place the lychees, reserved syrup, mint leaves, lime juice and ice cubes in a blender and blend until smooth. Pour into chilled glasses.

mint and ice cream smoothie

serves 2

250 g (9 oz/1 cup) vanilla ice cream
4 ice cubes
60 ml (2 fl oz/1/4 cup) crème de menthe
   (or other mint-flavoured liqueur)
6 mint leaves

Put the ice cream, ice cubes, crème de menthe and mint leaves in a blender. Blend until smooth, then pour the drink into small, chilled glasses.

classic daiquiri

serves 1

60 ml (2 fl oz/¼ cup) white rum
1 tablespoon lime juice
1 teaspoon Triple Sec
1 teaspoon caster (superfine) sugar
lime slices, to serve

Fill a cocktail shaker with ice and add the rum, lime juice, Triple Sec and caster sugar. Shake well and strain into a chilled cocktail glass. Serve with slices of lime.

mojito

4 sprigs mint
2 teaspoons sugar
1/2 lime, quartered
60 ml (2 fl oz/1/4 cup) white rum
4 ice cubes
soda water

Place the mint, sugar and lime in a glass and crush well with a muddler or the back of a wooden spoon. Add the rum and ice. Top with soda water.

tropical rum blend serves 2

30 ml (1 fl oz) white rum
30 ml (1 fl oz) Malibu
30 ml (1 fl oz) Midori
200 ml (7 fl oz) grapefruit juice
75 g (2$^1/_2$ oz/1 cup) peeled and roughly
   chopped honeydew melon
ice, to serve
honeydew melon wedges, to garnish

Place all the ingredients except the ice and honeydew wedges in a blender and blend until smooth. Pour into two tall glasses over ice and garnish with wedges of honeydew.

margarita

60 ml (2 fl oz/¼ cup) tequila
30 ml (1 fl oz) Triple Sec
1 tablespoon lime juice

Fill a shaker with ice and add the tequila, Triple Sec and lime juice. Shake vigorously. Wet the rim of a cocktail glass with lime and then dip it into sea salt. Strain the cocktail into the glass and serve.

martini

1 teaspoon dry vermouth
60 ml (2 fl oz/¹/4 cup) gin
olive or lemon peel, for garnish

Place a teaspoon of vermouth into a chilled martini glass. Fill a cocktail shaker with ice and add the gin. Swirl the vermouth around the glass, then pour it out. Strain the iced gin into the glass and serve immediately with a garnish of an olive or lemon peel.

mint julep

1¹/₂ teaspoons caster (superfine) sugar
10 mint leaves, plus extra, to garnish
110 g (4 oz/³/₄ cup) crushed ice
90 ml (3 fl oz) whisky

Place the sugar, six of the mint leaves and a dash of water in a glass. Using a muddler or the end of a wooden spoon, mash the ingredients together until the sugar is dissolved and the mint is bruised. Fill the glass with crushed ice and top with the whisky. Stir well and place in the freezer for 30 minutes. Serve with a garnish of mint leaves.

opal ice

220 g (8 oz/1 1/2 cups) crushed ice
30 ml (1 fl oz) white rum
30 ml (1 fl oz) Triple Sec
30 ml (1 fl oz) Midori
1 tablespoon lime juice
1 tablespoon blue Curaçao

Divide the ice between two large cocktail glasses. Place the rum, Triple Sec, Midori and lime juice in a cocktail shaker, add a little ice and shake well. Pour three-quarters of the blend into the two glasses, then add the Curaçao. Top with the remaining cocktail mix. Serve immediately.

moroccan mint tea   serves 1

4 sprigs mint
1 lemon wedge
1 star anise
1/2 cinnamon stick
1 teaspoon caster (superfine) sugar

Place the mint, lemon, star anise, cinnamon and sugar in a small glass and top with boiling water. Stir well to dissolve the sugar, and drink while hot.

lychee and rum blast serves 2

10 tinned lychees, seeded and chilled
80 ml (2¹/₂ fl oz/¹/₃ cup) coconut milk,
   chilled
60 ml (2 fl oz/¹/₄ cup) dark rum
60 ml (2 fl oz/¹/₄ cup) lychee syrup,
   chilled
10 mint leaves

Place all the ingredients in a blender
and blend until smooth. Pour into two
chilled glasses and serve immediately.

pesto stir-fry basics fresh mint sauce nori roll basics peanut dressing sweet ginger dressing lime and lemon grass dressing lemon and cumin dressing vinaigrette seafood marinade oatcakes walnut bread tamarind water chicken stock vegetable stock roast pork chicken marinade lime mayonnaise tomato rice shortcrust pastry case pesto stir-fry basics fresh mint sauce nori roll basics peanut dressing sweet

06 basics

ginger dressing lime and lemon grass dressing lemon and cumin dressing vinaigrette seafood marinade oatcakes walnut bread tamarind water chicken stock vegetable stock roast pork chicken marinade lime mayonnaise tomato rice shortcrust pastry case pesto

pesto

125 g (4^1/$_2$ oz) basil
1 handful flat-leaf (Italian) parsley
100 g (3^1/$_2$ oz/1 cup) grated fresh
   parmesan cheese
1 garlic clove
85 g (3 oz/^{1}/$_2$ cup) pine nuts, toasted
170 ml (5^1/$_2$ fl oz/^{2}/$_3$ cup) olive oil

Put the basil, parsley, parmesan cheese, garlic and toasted pine nuts in a food processor, or use a mortar and pestle. Blend together and add the olive oil in a steady stream until you have a spoonable consistency. Lightly toss the pesto through freshly cooked pasta and serve.

fresh mint sauce

makes 150 ml (5 fl oz)

1 handful mint leaves
2 teaspoons sugar
4 tablespoons apple cider vinegar

Put the mint on a chopping board, scatter with 1 teaspoon of the sugar, then finely chop. Transfer the mint to a serving bowl or jug and stir in the remaining sugar, 2 tablespoons of boiling water and the apple cider vinegar. Serve with grilled or roast lamb.

peanut dressing

makes 185 ml (6 fl oz/³/4 cup)

1 tablespoon shaved palm sugar (jaggery)
100 ml (3¹/2 fl oz) tamarind water (386)
2 tablespoons kecap manis
1 tablespoon balsamic vinegar
1 red chilli, seeded and finely chopped
1 garlic clove, finely chopped
70 g (2¹/2 oz/¹/2 cup) ground roasted peanuts

Combine the palm sugar, tamarind water, kecap manis and balsamic vinegar in a small bowl. Stir until the palm sugar has dissolved. Add the red chilli, garlic and peanuts. This dressing is delicious spooned over a salad of julienned vegetables or fresh tofu or thinly sliced beef with cucumber and mint.

sweet ginger dressing

makes 250 ml (9 fl oz/1 cup)

125 ml (4 fl oz/1/2 cup) dashi stock
3 tablespoons rice vinegar
4 tablespoons light soy sauce
3 teaspoons sugar
1 tablespoon finely grated fresh ginger

Put the dashi stock in a saucepan with the rice vinegar, light soy sauce and sugar. Bring to the boil, then remove from the heat and pour the hot liquid into a serving bowl. When the dressing has cooled, add the fresh ginger. This dressing is ideal for pouring over julienned vegetable salads or mixed salads that feature crab, prawns (shrimp) or other light seafood, as well as poached chicken.

lime and lemon grass dressing

makes 150 ml (5 fl oz)

4 tablespoons lime juice
4 tablespoons fish sauce
2 tablespoons sugar
2 tablespoons finely chopped lemon
   grass, white part only
1 garlic clove, very finely chopped
2 small red chillies, seeded and finely
   chopped

Put the lime juice, fish sauce and sugar into a bowl. Stir until the sugar has dissolved. Add the lemon grass, garlic and chillies. Stir to combine. This dressing is wonderful with seafood salads and simple salads of sliced cucumber, sprouts and fresh herbs. It can also be drizzled over chilled wedges of iceberg lettuce or poured over a rice noodle salad.

lemon and cumin dressing

makes 150 ml (5 fl oz)

2 tablespoons lemon juice
125 ml (4 fl oz/1/2 cup) olive oil
2 garlic cloves, very finely chopped
1 teaspoon ground cumin
large pinch of paprika

Combine the lemon juice, olive oil, garlic, cumin and paprika in a bowl and stir to blend.

This dressing is used on many Middle Eastern-style salads. Pour it over a salad of tomatoes and cucumbers or over lentils.

vinaigrette

80 ml (2^1/$_2$ fl oz/^{1}/$_3$ cup)

1 tablespoon lemon juice
3 tablespoons extra virgin olive oil
1 garlic clove
1 teaspoon finely chopped herbs such
  as tarragon, oregano, basil, chervil or
  thyme (optional)

Put the lemon juice and olive oil in a bowl and season with a pinch of sea salt and a grind of black pepper.

Bruise the garlic clove once with the wide blade of a large knife or a mallet. Add the garlic to the dressing, lightly stir and allow it to sit for 30 minutes to infuse. Remove the garlic, stir the dressing again, then use. You can also add herbs to the dressing.

Pour over salads that feature chicken or seafood.

seafood marinade

serves 4

1 teaspoon finely grated fresh ginger
2 tablespoons coriander (cilantro) leaves
2 tablespoons lime juice
3 tablespoons olive oil

Put the ginger, coriander, lime juice and olive oil into a bowl and stir to combine. Add the fish pieces. Toss the pieces in the marinade to ensure they are well coated. Allow to marinate in the refrigerator for 30 minutes before cooking.

chicken marinade

3 tablespoons lemon juice
3 tablespoons olive oil
1 tablespoon Dijon mustard
1 teaspoon finely chopped garlic
1 teaspoon thyme
1/2 teaspoon ground white pepper

Put the lemon juice, olive oil, Dijon mustard, garlic, thyme and pepper in a large bowl. Add the chicken pieces and toss to coat the pieces in the mixture, then marinate in the refrigerator for 2–3 hours.

Remove the chicken pieces from the marinade and barbecue or roast them until cooked. Season with sea salt and serve.

oatcakes

250 g (9 oz/2 cups) fine oatmeal, plus
extra, for rolling
1/2 teaspoon bicarbonate of soda
(baking soda)
30 g (1 oz) butter, melted

Preheat the oven to 160°C (315°F/ Gas 2–3). Mix together the oatmeal, bicarbonate of soda and 1/2 teaspoon of salt. Add the butter and 150 ml (5 fl oz) of hot water. Stir well to form a soft dough. Knead gently for 1 minute. Divide the dough into four portions. Roll out one portion thinly between two sheets of baking paper. Using a 3–4 cm (11/4–11/2 in) round cookie cutter, cut the dough into small rounds. Repeat with the remaining portions of dough. Place the rounds on a lined baking tray. Bake for 15 minutes, or until pale and dry. Cool.

walnut bread

1 teaspoon dry yeast powder
1 teaspoon sugar
185 g (6 1/2 oz/1 1/2 cups) plain (all-purpose) flour
30 g (1 oz/1/4 cup) finely chopped walnuts
1 tablespoon walnut oil

Mix the yeast, sugar and 125 ml (4 fl oz/1/2 cup) of warm water in a bowl. Cover and leave in a warm place for 10 minutes, or until frothy. Place the flour, walnuts and 1/4 teaspoon of salt in a bowl. Make a well in the centre and add the yeast mixture. Mix to form a dough, gather into a ball, then turn out onto a floured surface and knead until smooth. Transfer to a large bowl brushed with walnut oil. Cover and leave in a warm place for 1 hour, or until doubled in size. Punch down, halve the mixture and shape each portion into a sausage shape 23 cm long x 3 cm thick (9 in x 1 1/4 in). Twist each sausage to form a loose spiral and place on a greased baking tray. Cover and leave in a warm place for 40 minutes, or until doubled in size. Preheat the oven to 180°C (350°F/Gas 4). Bake for 25 minutes, or until golden and hollow-sounding when tapped. Cool. Slice each loaf into 5 mm (1/4 in) slices, cutting on a diagonal. Reduce the oven to 160°C (315°F/Gas 2–3). Place the slices on a baking tray and return to the oven for 8 minutes, or until crisp. Allow to cool.

vegetable stock

makes about 2 litres (70 fl oz/8 cups)

40 g (1¹/2 oz) unsalted butter
2 garlic cloves, crushed
2 onions, roughly chopped
4 leeks, coarsely chopped
3 carrots, coarsely chopped
3 celery stalks, thickly sliced
1 fennel bulb, trimmed, coarsely
  chopped
1 handful flat-leaf (Italian) parsley
2 sprigs thyme
2 black peppercorns

Put the butter, garlic and onions into a large, heavy-based saucepan. Put the pan over medium heat and stir until the onion is soft and transparent. Add the leeks, carrots, celery stalks, fennel bulb, parsley, thyme and peppercorns. Add 4 litres (140 fl oz/ 16 cups) of water and bring to the boil. Reduce the heat and simmer for 2 hours. Allow to cool. Strain into another saucepan, using the back of a large spoon to press the liquid from the vegetables. Bring the stock to the boil, then reduce the heat to a rolling boil until the stock is reduced by half. If you are not using the stock immediately, cover and refrigerate or freeze it.

chicken stock

makes about 2 litres (70 fl oz/8 cups)

1 whole fresh chicken
1 onion, sliced
2 celery stalks, sliced
1 leek, roughly chopped
1 bay leaf
a few flat-leaf (Italian) parsley stalks
6 peppercorns

Fill a large heavy-based saucepan with 3 litres (105 fl oz/12 cups) of cold water. Cut the chicken into several large pieces and put them into the pan. Bring just to the boil, then reduce the heat to a simmer. Skim any fat from the surface, then add the onion, celery stalks, leek, bay leaf, parsley stalks and peppercorns. Maintain the heat at a low simmer for 2 hours. Strain the stock into a bowl and allow to cool. Using a large spoon, remove any fat that has risen to the surface. If a more concentrated flavour is required, return the stock to a saucepan and simmer over low heat. If you are not using the stock immediately, cover and refrigerate or freeze it.

lemon mayonnaise   serves 4

2 egg yolks
1 lemon, zested and juiced
250 ml (9 fl oz/1 cup) oil

Whisk the egg yolks, lemon zest and juice together in a large bowl. Slowly drizzle in the oil while whisking until the mixture thickens, and keep whisking the mixture until it becomes thick and creamy. Season to taste with sea salt. If the mixture is very thick, add a little cold water until you achieve the right consistency.

lime mayonnaise

2 egg yolks
1 lime, zested and juiced
250 ml (9 fl oz/1 cup) oil

Whisk the egg yolks, lime zest and juice together in a large bowl. Slowly drizzle in the oil while whisking until the mixture thickens, and keep whisking the mixture until it becomes thick and creamy. Season to taste with sea salt. If the mixture is very thick, add a little cold water until you achieve the right consistency.

tomato rice

1 tablespoon sesame oil
1 onion, finely diced
1 garlic clove, crushed
3 ripe tomatoes, diced
200 g (7 oz/1 cup) basmati rice

Put the sesame oil in a large saucepan over medium heat. Add the onion and garlic and cook until the onion is soft and transparent. Add the tomatoes, rice and $1/2$ teaspoon sea salt and stir for a minute before adding 375 ml ($1 1/2$ cups) of water. Raise the heat and bring the rice to the boil. Cover the saucepan with a lid and reduce the heat to low. Leave covered for 20 minutes and then remove from the heat.

mashed potato

4 large floury potatoes, peeled
2 tablespoons milk
40 g (1 1/2 oz) butter

Cut the potatoes into pieces and cook them in simmering water for 15 minutes, or until they are soft. Drain well. Put them back in the pan with the milk and butter and mash them until they are smooth. Season with sea salt and freshly cracked black pepper.

tamarind water

makes 500 ml (17 fl oz/2 cups)

100 g (3¹/₂ oz) tamarind pulp

To make tamarind water, put the tamarind pulp in a bowl and cover it with 500 ml (2 cups) of boiling water. Allow it to steep for 1 hour, stirring occasionally to break up the fibres, then strain.

shortcrust tart case

makes 1 tart case

200 g (7 oz/1²/₃ cups) plain (all-purpose) flour
100 g (3¹/₂ oz) unsalted butter
1 tablespoon caster (superfine) sugar

Put the flour, butter, sugar and a pinch of salt into a food processor and process for 1 minute. Add 2 tablespoons of chilled water and pulse until the mixture comes together. Wrap the dough in plastic wrap and chill for 30 minutes.

Roll the pastry out as thinly as possible. The easiest way to do this is to roll it out between two layers of plastic wrap. Line a greased 25 cm (10 in) tart tin. Chill for a further 30 minutes. Prick the base, line it with crumpled greaseproof paper and fill with rice or baking weights. Place the tin in a preheated 180°C (350°F/ Gas 4) oven for 10 to 15 minutes, or until the pastry looks cooked and dry. Remove and allow to cool.

Note – Tart cases that are not used immediately can be stored in the freezer for several weeks. Put the tart case in a preheated oven direct from the freezer (there's no need to thaw the case first).

glossary

balsamic vinegar

Balsamic vinegar is a dark, fragrant, sweetish aged vinegar made from grape juice. The production of authentic balsamic vinegar is controlled. Bottles of the real thing have 'Aceto Balsamico Tradizionale de Modena' written on the label.

basil

The most commonly used basil is the sweet or Genoa variety which is much favoured in Italian cooking. Thai or holy basil is used in Thai and South-East Asian dishes. To get the most out of basil leaves they should always be torn not chopped.

betel leaves

These are the aromatic, lacy-edged green leaves from the betel pepper. They can be found in Indian shops.

black sesame seeds

Mainly used in Asian cooking, black sesame seeds add colour, crunch and a distinct nuttiness to whatever dish they garnish. They can be found in most Asian grocery stores.

bocconcini

These are small balls of mozzarella, often sold sitting in their own whey. When fresh they are soft and springy to the touch and taste distinctly milky. They are available from most delicatessens.

capers

Capers are preserved in brine or salt. Salted capers have a firmer texture. Rinse away the brine or salt before using them.

Chinese black beans

These salted black beans can be found either vacuum-packed or in tins in Asian food stores.

Chinese rice wine

The wine is similar to a fine sherry and is made from glutinous rice. It is often used in braised dishes and sauces.

choy sum

Also known as flowering Chinese cabbage. It has mid-green leaves and tender stems.

coconut cream

Slightly thicker than coconut milk, coconut cream is available in tins. If you can't get hold of it, use the thick cream off the top of a couple of tins of coconut milk instead.

crème fraîche

A naturally soured cream which is lighter than sour cream, it is available at gourmet food stores and some large supermarkets.

daikon

Daikon, or mooli, is a large white radish. Its flavour varies from mild to quite spicy. It can be freshly grated or slow-cooked in broths, and is available from most large supermarkets.

dried Asian fried onions

Crisp-fried shallots or onions are available from most Asian grocery stores and are normally packaged in plastic tubs or bags. They are often used as a flavour enhancer, scattered over rice and savoury dishes.

feta cheese

Feta is a white cheese made from sheep's milk or goat's milk. The fresh cheese is salted and cut into blocks before being matured in its own whey. It must be kept in the whey or in oil during storage. Feta is available from delicatessens and most supermarkets.

fish sauce

This is a highly flavoured, salty liquid made from fermented fish and widely used in South Asian cuisine to give a salty, savoury flavour. Buy a small bottle and keep it in the fridge.

ginger juice

Fresh ginger juice is produced by finely grating fresh ginger and then squeezing the liquid from the grated flesh.

haloumi cheese

Haloumi is a semi-firm sheep's milk cheese. It has a rubbery texture which becomes soft and chewy when the cheese is grilled or fried. It is available from delicatessens and most large supermarkets.

Indian lime pickle

Lime pickle is available from Indian grocery stores or large supermarkets. It is usually served as a side dish in Indian cooking.

lemon grass

These long fragrant stems are very popular in Thai cuisine. The tough outer layers should be stripped off first and it can then be used either finely chopped or whole in soups. Lemon grass can be stored for up to 2 weeks.

makrut leaves

Also known as the kaffir lime, the glossy leaves of this South-East Asian tree impart a wonderful citrusy aroma.

mesclun

Mesclun is a green salad mix originating in Provence, France. This salad often contains a selection of young, small leaves.

mint

Mint comes in many different varieties including peppermint, spearmint and applemint, but the common garden variety is wonderful in salads or as a garnish.

mirin

Mirin is a rice wine used in Japanese cooking. It adds sweetness to many sauces and dressings, and is used for marinating and glazing dishes like teriyaki. It is available from Asian grocery stores and large supermarkets.

mizuna

These tender young salad leaves have a pleasant, peppery flavour

mozzarella cheese

Fresh mozzarella can be found in most delicatessens and is easily identified by its smooth, white appearance and ball-like shape.

nori

Nori is an edible seaweed sold in paper-thin sheets. To concentrate the flavour, lightly roast the shiny side of the sheets over a low flame. Nori sheets are available from most large supermarkets and Asian grocery stores.

orange flower water

This perfumed distillation of bitter-orange blossoms is mostly used as a flavouring in baked goods and drinks. It is available from delicatessens and large supermarkets.

oyster sauce

Made from oysters, brine and soy sauce, this thick brown sauce is a popular Asian seasoning.

palm sugar

Palm sugar is obtained from the sap of various palm trees and is sold in hard cakes or cylinders and in plastic jars. It can be found in Asian grocery stores or large supermarkets. Substitute with soft brown sugar if unavailable.

pancetta

Pancetta is salted belly of pork. It is sold in good delicatessens, especially Italian ones, and some supermarkets. Pancetta is available either rolled and finely sliced or in large pieces ready to be diced or roughly cut. It adds a rich bacon flavour to dishes.

panettone

An aromatic Italian yeast bread made with raisins and candied peel, panettone is traditionally eaten at Christmas, when it is found in Italian delicatessens or large supermarkets.

papaya

This large tropical fruit can be orange, red or yellow. This fruit contains an enzyme which will stop gelatine from setting so avoid using it in any jellies. Sometimes called a pawpaw, they are really part of the custard apple family.

pesto

Available ready-made in most supermarkets, pesto is a puréed sauce traditionally made from basil, garlic, Parmesan cheese, pine nuts and olive oil.

pickled ginger

Japanese pickled ginger is available from most large supermarkets. The thin slivers of young ginger root are pickled in sweet vinegar and turn a distinctive salmon-pink colour inthe process. The vinegar adds a sweet, gingery bite.

pink peppercorns

These are not true peppercorns but rather are the aromatic dried red berries from the tree *Schinus molle*. They have an aromatic peppery flavour.

preserved lemon

These are whole lemons preserved in salt or brine, which turns their rind soft and pliable. Just the rind is used. It is available from delicatessens.

prosciutto

Prosciutto is lightly salted, air-dried ham. It is most commonly bought in paper-thin slices, and is available from delicatessens and large supermarkets. Parma ham and San Daniele are both types of prosciutto.

rice paper

Edible rice paper sheets are available from most large supermarkets or speciality cookware shops. The thin sheets are most commonly used to wrap nougat and panforte.

rice paper wrappers

Rice paper wrappers are predominantly used in the cuisines of Vietnam and Thailand. They are made of rice and water paste and come in thin, round or square sheets, which soften when soaked in water. Use to wrap around food. They are available in most large supermarkets or from speciality Asian stores.

rice wine vinegar

Made from fermented rice, this vinegar comes in clear, red and black versions. If no colour is specified in a recipe, use the clear vinegar. The clear rice wine vinegar is sweeter and milder than its European counterparts or the sharper flavoured Chinese black vinegar.

risoni

Risoni are small rice-shaped pasta. They are ideal for use in soups or salads.

risotto rice

There are three well-known varieties of risotto rice that are widely available: arborio, a large plump grain that makes a stickier risotto; vialone nano, a shorter grain that gives a loose consistency but keeps more of a bite in the middle; and carnaroli, which makes a risotto with a firm consistency.

saffron threads

Saffron should be bought in small quantities and used sparingly — not only due to the cost but as it has a very strong flavour. Beware of inexpensive brands when buying saffron, as cheap, real saffron does not exist!

sashimi salmon

Salmon sold for making sushi and sashimi, which is intended to be eaten raw, is usually the freshest fish at the market. Buy a thick piece cut from the centre rather than a narrower tail end.

sesame oil

Sesame oil is available in two varieties. The darker, more pungent, type is made with roasted sesame seeds and comes from China, while a paler, non-roasted variety is Middle Eastern in origin.

shiitake mushrooms

These Asian mushrooms have white gills and a brown cap. Meaty in texture, they keep their shape very well when cooked. Dried shiitake are often sold as dried Chinese mushrooms.

sichuan pepper

Made from the dried red berries of the prickly ash tree, the flavour is spicy-hot and leaves a numbing aftertaste, which can linger. Dry-fry and crush the berries for the best flavour.

tofu

This white curd is made from soya beans. Bland in taste, it takes on the flavour of the other ingredients. Usually sold in blocks, there are several different types of tofu — soft (silken), firm, sheets and deep-fried. Refrigerate fresh tofu covered in water for up to five days, changing the water daily.

Vietnamese mint

Vietnamese mint is actually not really a true mint. Also known as hot mint or laksa mint, its spicy flavour is usually found paired with spring rolls and laksas.

wakame

Wakame is a seaweed that is most commonly sold in its dried form. It must be soaked in warm water until it softens and is most commonly used in salads and soups.

wasabi

Mostly sold in tubes or in a powdered dried form (mixed to a paste with a little water). It has a very hot flavour. Used to flavour sushi, sashimi or some sauces.

water chesnuts

The edible tuber of a water plant, the water chestnut is white and crunchy and adds a delicate texture to many South-East Asian dishes. Fresh water chestnuts can be bought at Chinese food stores, but they are commonly available whole or sliced in tins.

witlof

Also called Belgian endive or chicory, this salad leaf has a bitter flavour and crisp, crunchy texture when raw. You can find witlof in both pale yellow and purple varieties.

wonton wrappers

These paper-thin sheets of dough are available either fresh or frozen from Asian grocery stores. They may be wrapped around fillings and steamed, deep-fried or used in broths. The wrappers come shaped both as squares and circles.

index